Living Next to Paradise

# Living Next to Paradise

*A Memoir by Diana Raphael*

### Edited by Liz Griffin

*Living Next to Paradise*
Diana Raphael
Edited by Liz Griffin

Designed, printed and bound by Aspect Design
89 Newtown Road, Malvern, Worcs. WR14 1PD
United Kingdom
Tel: 01684 561567
E-mail: allan@aspect-design.net
Website: www.aspect-design.net

All Rights Reserved.

Copyright © 2024 Diana Raphael

The right of Diana Raphael to be identified as the author of this work has been asserted in accordance with Section 77 of the Copyright, Designs and Patents Act 1988.

Diana Raphael has asserted her moral right to be identified as the author of this work.

This book is sold subject to the condition that it shall not, by way of trade or otherwise, be lent, resold, hired out or otherwise circulated without the publisher's prior consent in any form of binding or cover other than that in which it is published and without a similar condition including this condition being imposed on the subsequent purchaser.

A copy of this book has been deposited
with the British Library Board
Cover design Copyright © 2024 Aspect Design

ISBN 978-1-916919-19-8

## List of Illustrations

Me and my dad .................................................... vi
Map of Evesham .................................................. 2
Mum and Dad on their wedding day ................................. 5
An early photo of the Ferry........................................ 8
Afternoon tea by the river proved popular ........................... 17
Me with some of Mum's famous bread pudding ...................... 21
Dad with his pigeons .............................................. 31
A harsh winter on the Avon ........................................ 41
The new café ..................................................... 46
Avonbank Brass Band ............................................. 49
The wedding party crossing by Ferry for TV.......................... 68
And our official photograph later that day ........................... 69
Sam and our three boys: John, Jamie and Scott....................... 78
My dad, Ernest Huxley, in typical pose .............................. 83
The new cafe with three generations, in 1978 ........................ 86
Mayor of Evesham................................................ 102
Meeting Princess Anne ............................................ 104
Meeting Princess Margaret ......................................... 104
My parents' golden wedding with their Ferryboys .................... 108
A new boat in 1984 and the old ferry was filled with flowers ........... 113
Next to Paradise .................................................. 117

Me and my dad. Most Sunday evenings Dad would take the dogs for a walk and say to Mum: 'I am going to view the estate,' always saying on his return: 'I have just been to Paradise, it is so peaceful and quiet down there I love it.' From then on it was always known by us all as Paradise.

# Introduction

In the early 700s, Ecgwin, the Bishop of Worcester, was made aware of a swineherd called Eof, who had had a vision of the Virgin Mary as he tended his pigs on the Hamm.

Ecgwin visited the place and he too saw the vision of the Virgin Mary and took it as a sign he should build an abbey. When asked where it was to be, he said Eofs-Hamm now known as Evesham.

The Abbey was built and grew into a rich Benedictine monastery, occupying very fertile soil, where every food the monks needed could be grown – including grapes for their wine. The vineyard was planted on a hillside on the opposite bank of the river Avon but, to tend it, the monks had to walk almost two miles each way, as there was only one bridge over the river.

So, in the eleventh century, to make it easier and quicker, a ferry crossing over the river was created with a building for making and storing wine. And this is the origin of Hampton Ferry.

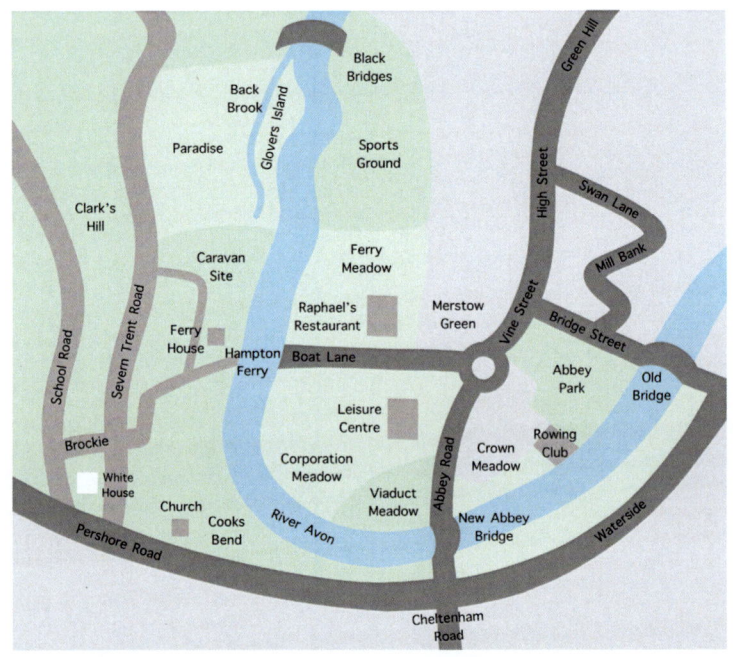

Map of Evesham showing 'Paradise', drawn by Alexandra Munro

## Chapter One
## Moving in (1929)

It was Sunday, 29 September and twenty-five-year-old Eileen was cycling as hard as she could. She was full of anticipation for her new life with her husband of almost a year, but her face was not just wet from the rain. It was mixed with tears as she thought about her family she was leaving behind in Birmingham.

But pretty Eileen was full of energy and had been waiting for this moment for months. It was time to plan for the future. Knowing how much she would miss the happy home on the Coventry Road and parents William and Kate, sister Grace and brothers George and Wellesley, she determined to have a phone installed in her new home as soon as possible. That would be easier than writing and make it quicker to tell her folks all her news.

She hadn't yet been inside the house, but it certainly looked big and impressive, and she could hardly wait to see what it was like inside.

Only a few miles more and she would find out . . .

Eileen had met the love of her life, Ernest William Huxley, in 1927, on a week's holiday with a girlfriend in the small market town of Evesham. Ernest was twenty-four then and a handsome five-foot-six to Eileen's pleasantly plump five-foot. She was smitten, the romance blossomed, and, on 1 December 1928, they married in Yardley Old Church near her parents' home in Birmingham.

They had already been looking for somewhere to live for months so when the lease on Hampton Ferry became available, Ernest was determined – this is where he wanted to spend the rest of his life. He started negotiations with the Rudge Estate but there were conditions: they would not lease to a single man. So Eileen and Ernie arranged to bring forward their marriage but still had to observe another condition – the twelve-month notice period before the lease could be taken up, so the couple were married for almost a year before setting up house together.

As they couldn't afford to buy anywhere in the meantime, Eileen stayed with her parents in Birmingham and Ernie with his, in Evesham. Both were working and saving hard. Eileen worked in an office for a Mr Jarvis who had played a key role in starting the football pools. She sent out his letters and, when they were returned, filed them alphabetically. She proved a dab hand at this and quick, earning 21 shillings a week (£1.10p). And Ernie was the captain of the *Jubilee Queen*, taking home 10/6d a week (52 & half pence) for taking river trips up and down the Avon during summer weekends, while also serving as an apprentice nurseryman, for five shillings (25pence) during the week.

He was the second child of Rose and Edmund Huxley. Their firstborn was Edmund Thomas (always known as Pat), born in the house at the bottom of Bridge Street in the Fleece Yard Evesham, as were Ernest and his nine brothers and sisters. They all knew Evesham well and Ernie's love of the river and boats had been born when, at just nine years-old, he got a Saturday job on the ferry starting a long friendship with the then Ferryman Mr Welland.

During their courtship and for the year after their wedding, Eileen had cycled from Birmingham to Evesham for the weekends and, occasionally, usually during the winter months, Ernest did the travelling and, as Eileen's bottom drawer filled with things for the new home that she bought or been given, he travelled by train to carry heavier things and the well-packed suitcases back to Evesham.

On one occasion, she gave him a box containing her wedding dress, hat, and shoes. Being clever with a needle and crochet hook she had crocheted her own wedding dress and hat and looked lovely in them on her wedding day. She realised she would probably not

Mum and Dad on their wedding day – she's wearing her beautiful dress

wear them again but was justifiably proud of her beautiful creations. Ernie, however, unfortunately left the box on the train and, despite his best efforts, failed to find it. He also failed to tell Eileen. When she asked about the box several months later, there were not only a few words, but he was never allowed to forget he had lost her wedding dress . . .

But that was to come and now, on this momentous day, she was at last cycling down Greenhill into Evesham, the town she was already thinking of as home – slower paced and friendly. With her laden bicycle, a small suitcase in the front basket along with a few packages, and the panniers bursting with her clothes and shoes. She couldn't wait to get indoors, out of the rain and maybe into a nice hot bath, or, at least some dry clothes.

Ernie was anxiously waiting in the Ferry House for her arrival and as excited as she when she cycled down Boat Lane. Hastily they put her bicycle on the Ferry and Ernie pulled the rope until they reached the other side. Eileen, full of high expectations, eagerly went into the house. She found herself in a big front room with a lovely bay window but completely empty except for a roaring fire in a huge black range. There were two ovens one on either side of the fire and a big black cauldron filled with water hung over the flames. The floor's grey flagstones glistened and winked at her.

But a closer inspection of the room she would come to know as The Lounge dampened her relief. Literally. The flagstones were not glistening with polish but with moisture and reflecting the flames from the fire. Not only that, but there was grass growing between the stones. Eileen could hardly believe her eyes.

Ernie sensed that she was not best pleased and, hugging her, said: 'Come on, I will show you the rest of the house.' In the kitchen, there was a big boiler across one corner with a fireplace underneath to boil water for a bath or on wash day. In the other corner a square pantry, filled with shelves but with plenty of space to keep things cool and out of sight. It was a peculiar shape, with the pantry in one corner, next to it there was a Belfast sink with a tap, but no water. The water boiler was diagonally across the room but there was room for a table and chairs, when they could afford them.

She was led into the little room which became known as the dining room. There was a door in and on the left, another door which opened on to the stairs. These were narrow, steep and curved. She would have liked to explore upstairs, but the way was blocked . . . Ernest explained he and his brother Bob had been trying to get upstairs with the big brass bedstead – a wedding present from Eileen's parents – when it got stuck. Bob was trapped upstairs and could not get down, but an extra pair of hands should solve it.

A lengthy spell of pushing and pulling by all three made no difference and, finally they gave up, moving the bed downstairs into the lounge – a good idea as it was by far the warmest room in the house.

Eileen continued her tour, finding three bedrooms upstairs: one very small, one a bit bigger and one over the lounge that was quite a nice size. It was decidedly damp, cold and smelled musty. Each bedroom had a fireplace, and she was sure a fire would cure the damp and the smell.

But going back downstairs a thought struck her. Where was the bathroom or toilet? Was there running water in the kitchen? When she asked Ernie, he reluctantly admitted there was only a wooden privy in the garden. For water, there was a tap outside with a bucket under it. Said Ernie: 'We can't turn it on or off – it just drips – so we leave a bucket and when we need water, we usually have a bucket full.' Ernie had known all this from working on the ferry for several years but had not thought to tell Eileen.

She was cold, tired, and hungry. She was in a house, primitive to say the least, having left one with electric light, running water, inside toilet, gas cooker and all mod cons. She'd also quit a good job to come to this damp, cold, barn of a place in the middle of nowhere. Eileen sat down on one of the boxes stacked in the dining room and burst into tears.

But Ernie put his arms around her, held her close and reassured her quietly about how wonderful it was going to be when it had been fixed up, and what a fantastic place it would be to bring up children. They were going to be so happy

An early photo of the Ferry, showing the fares

By this time, Bob was cooking bacon and eggs over the big fire in the Lounge and the smell of which was wonderful. Soon all three of them were sitting on the bed, eating a feast fit for a king and the world looked a decidedly better place as Ernie took Bob across the Ferry for him to go home.

And that brought more good news, as he counted the day's takings. The fare was one halfpenny return and they had taken six shillings and three pence halfpenny – equal to 153 people crossing. Eileen brightened even more at the thought that, at this rate, they could afford what needed doing on the house. Ernest didn't have the heart to tell her many of the customers had come out of curiosity to see who had taken over the Ferry so it would not always be as busy. He would leave that for her to find out for herself.

## Chapter Two

## Improvements

Eileen was amazed how quickly she settled to her new life in the country even though it was so very different from living in Birmingham. Making her house comfortable as soon as possible was a priority so she found a plumber to look at the tap that only dripped.

When he arrived, he got a spanner, took off the tap and removed a round marble-sized stone that had been sitting snugly inside. Tap back on and, like magic, the sink now had running water. He only asked for a cup of tea in return because the job had been so simple. Eileen was delighted. Running water would make such a difference.

Next on her list was the wooden privy outside. She had cleaned it thoroughly, added some sweeter smelling stuff down the hole and threaded newspaper on a string for use as loo paper. Now she discussed the possibility of having a bathroom installed inside. The plumber agreed it was possible but warned of the cost, as it would mean putting in a cess pit, particularly if she wanted a bath.

A bathroom was not high on Ernie's priority list. He was sure they could continue to manage with the big tin bath, carried in from outside to the Lounge. Filled with hot water, they could both bathe in front of a roaring fire – a romantic arrangement Ernie quite liked. Eileen was not averse to it either, but she longed for some privacy and the ease of turning on a hot tap.

But a new bathroom moved down the list and was not to be

installed for a few years. One of the first improvements was the floor. The big flagstone slabs were removed and replaced with the then popular Marley tiles. Mr Cox was the builder and, loath to throw away the grey flagstones, used them in the Almonry Museum when it was being repaired. (Years later the family always felt at home in the museum, knowing the floor was from the house where they grew up.)

Bob, Ernie's brother, was a coal man and would sometimes drop off a bag of coal and, with plenty of trees around, they were never short of fuel for the ever-hungry fires in the house. The big brass bed stayed in the front room for almost a year and, as they had no furniture to speak of, it didn't matter. It was finally moved out of the Lounge when new windows were being installed upstairs and they were able to take the bed in through a bedroom window.

Gradually the house was furnished. Eileen's parents had given them a few odds and ends of furniture: some chests of drawers and a huge wardrobe with drawers and hanging space. It had to be taken to pieces and carried upstairs, to be re-assembled in the bedroom, a task that required a proper carpenter.

Two chairs had been bought at E. G. Righton's auction at the Smithfield Market: a Parker Knoll leather rocking chair Ernie claimed as his and an upright Queen Anne-style chair Eileen was delighted with. They had a three-penny bit table from Eileen's parents, four assorted chairs and a long low sideboard on legs.

A natural homemaker and clever with a needle, Eileen had soon made curtains for the rooms and rag rugs for the floor so, with the new tiles it all looked so much better – cosy and very comfortable.

Ernie contributed too. He had frequently run the Ferry for

Mr Welland before taking over completely and, when the New Bridge was being built at Evesham, the river had flooded while he was in charge. The flood water carried the partly-built bridge downstream where it got caught on the ferry rope. Ernie managed to tie it to a tree, saving at least part of it. When he told Evesham Borough Council, they gratefully retrieved it and gave him a reward of 10/6p (fifty-two and a half pence) which bolstered the couple's home-building efforts.

In the kitchen, Eileen managed to do a lot of the cooking on a gas stove and was adept at making bread and cakes every day in the ovens on the side of the range in the Lounge. Ernie had acquired a few chickens and ducks, so they were well supplied with eggs. They also had a goat, which Ernie milked for some quite lucrative orders from people allergic to cow's milk.

He also acquired a pig, which they called Lucy. She became such a tame family pet Eileen couldn't bear the thought of eating her. Instead, Lucy was mated and produced a litter of piglets almost every year which kept Hampton Ferry well supplied with pork and bacon.

Eileen boiled up all the leftovers, cabbage leaves, potato peelings and waste food in a big pot of water over the fire every day to feed them. Many a visitor commented on the enticing smell and Eileen would always invite them to share the pigs' tea – if they really wished.

The couple often related the story of the day Lucy wandered off and up into the village of Hampton where several men chased her all over the place trying to catch her. When Ernie discovered Lucy was missing, he went looking for her. Hearing her squeal, he soon discovered her with the men all looking very hot and bothered as they struggled to hold on to her. They were a bit put out when Ernie asked for her back, as they had had other plans, but Ernie rattled the pig bucket he was holding, Lucy gave an extra wriggle, and broke lose. She then followed Ernie home like a dog, much to the amazement of the small crowd that had gathered to see what was happening.

The piglets were usually sold but they would always keep one or two to use when they had grown bigger.

The pig-killing was a big event. A man from the abattoir arrived to kill the pig humanely, then it was hung up by its feet to drain the blood and the hairs were singed off. People from Hampton started to arrive, bringing their pots, pans, and jugs to soon return home with blood, chitterlings, pigs' feet, liver, heart, kidneys. etc. (Not many people owned freezers in those days).

The butcher would cut the meat into portions: some to be sold, some to eat that day and some to hang from the rafters in the Lounge where, every day Eileen would cure the sides of bacon by rubbing in various spices. Ernie often said the only unsellable thing on a pig was its squeal – everything else was used. When the bacon was cured, it would be sliced, keeping the family provided with many meals. As there was no electricity, a Tilly lamp always hung in the middle of the Lounge and went some way to smoke the bacon.

This Tilley lamp also gained a distinctive smell at Christmas. Sammy Grove always gave Ernie a bottle of whisky as a 'thank you' for dropping the Ferry rope while his steamers went by.

Ernie, in his youth, got exceedingly drunk one Christmas and 'lost' two whole days, frightening him so much he never touched alcohol again. So, although grateful for the bottle, he wouldn't drink it, instead pouring it into the Tilley lamp instead of paraffin, to provide light over Christmas. Now, the smell of burning whisky brings back the festive season for the family. Some of Ernie's brothers regretted the waste so he offered to swap the whisky for a bottle of paraffin, but they never did.

## Chapter Three
## Making Ends Meet

It wasn't just a home they were creating but a sound foundation for their business life. Eileen and Ernie were very happy, working hard to make ends meet. Ernie put his skills as a nurseryman to good use, making garden frames, putting up a greenhouse and doing quite well selling flower and vegetable plants during the week, in between manning the Ferry.

At weekends he worked for Sammy Grove, driving one of the steamers, so it was left to Eileen to look after the Ferry as well as serve and sell the plants. Luckily, Ernie had lots of brothers and sisters who rallied round and helped while the young boys in Hampton were always keen to do the Ferry and earn a copper or two. Now, at the top of the Brocky (footpath from Hampton to the Ferry called Broad Close which, in Evesham dialect became Brauclaus then shortened to The Brocky) on School Road lived Mr Clapson, an elderly master carpenter who liked wood and loved working with it, regretting his retirement.

He had first got to know the couple when he was called in to assist with the wardrobe re-assembly, starting a life-long friendship. After the wardrobe he made shelves here and there for them before the realisation of a great dream – making punts. These long, wooden, narrow boats, propelled by a man using a long pole, were to be rented by people intent on spending a lazy hour or so on the river.

They were beautiful and well-made to hold six very comfortably with two couples sitting in the bottom of the flat boat facing each other, another at the front with a paddle and another at the end with the pole.

When the punts were being built, Eileen set about making them even more comfortable with big soft cushions, stuffed with the feathers she had accumulated from the frequent duck /chicken/ goose that featured on their menu.

The boats were a huge success and much in demand from folks' intent on a relaxing sunny afternoon on the river. Charging a penny farthing an hour (3p), they soon paid for themselves. Mr Clapson started with two but soon there were twelve punts, numbered and tied up in numerical order on a newly-built landing-stage just upstream of the Ferry.

Ernie was very good at poling and paddling the punts, as was his younger brother Jim. They enjoyed impromptu races upriver and then back down. The skill needed to win was in the turning round...

Ever one to try and increase their income, Eileen started serving tea out of the kitchen window to the visitors who came to buy Ernie's plants and to the people who hired the punts. To start with, it was just a cup of tea, but it soon grew into an afternoon tea of two boiled eggs, bread and butter, a slice of fruit cake and a pot of tea. This feast, in the early 1930s, cost the princely sum of 1/- or 5p in today's money.

Ernie also had the idea of mowing the big meadow which lay from the house up towards Cook's bend and here he laid out a perfect putting green. This was not easy. The ground had to be dug over, rolled and then planted with grass seed so it was a full

## Chapter Three

twelve months before Ernie could put out the putting green.

When the grass grew long it had to be cut, using a wide push-mower and a huge garden scythe. Although Ernie was extremely skilled at this, he wasn't as good as Tom Pinchin, a man Ernie employed on a regular basis to keep the grass mown. Swiftly, the putting green brought even more people to Hampton Ferry attracted by an afternoon's entertainment: a trip on the river, a round of putting and Eileen's afternoon tea served from her

Afternoon tea by the river proved popular

kitchen window before finally buy some flowers to plant at home. It proved idyllic and they were kept busy when the weather was good – but that wasn't always the case.

Winter was always hard, with no income to speak of from the Ferry, so every Christmas for the first ten years at Hampton Ferry, Eileen would borrow £10 from her mother and, during the summer she would repay it. Neither her father nor Ernie ever knew of this and it was only confided to Diana in later years.

But, despite the hard work, Eileen and Ernie were delighted with their new life and ready to start a family. In February 1933, their first daughter was born, Deirdre Shirley Spencer Huxley As their house still had no proper bathroom, Eileen went home to her parents in Birmingham to have her baby. Here, she found time to sit and read, thoroughly enjoyed the relaxation. A heroine in one of the books she read then was Deirdre, Countess Rocklitz. This story delighted Deirdre later, especially when she realised the reason why they had a dog called Rocklitz – she was grateful they had named her Deirdre.

An addition to the family was a golden Cocker spaniel, that started the Huxley tradition of calling their dogs Rocklitz. Over the years, they must have had five or six dogs – all Cocker spaniels, which Ernie trained and bred from, providing the family with not only a pet but a small income when puppies arrived.

Eileen put her foot down, insisting she would not return to Hampton Ferry with the new baby until a bathroom and a telephone had been installed. This time, it worked. Plans were made, people consulted, and work started. In the process the kitchen was made smaller, and a wall put up to make the bathroom and toilet private. In no time at all they had an inside loo and a private bathroom.

So, no more walking up the garden path on a cold winter night. Sheer bliss and, how wonderful to have, at last, a proper bath. Obviously, there had to be a snag. There was no hot running water. All the water still had to be heated in the boiler in the kitchen or on the cauldron on the fire in the front room. It wasn't ideal, but for Eileen, a big improvement.

The telephone was positioned in the new hallway. Its number

was 58, then 458, then 2,458 and, many years later, 442,458. On the wall by the phone was left a glorious space on which to write phone numbers and, for many years, Eileen never allowed anyone to decorate there.

Businesses, friends and, especially, emergency numbers could always be found quickly. One corner was specifically kept for the numbers of people who lived on the riverbank so they could be warned of impending floods.

Mr Frank Watkins was their next-door neighbour and lived in a small bungalow a few yards away, separated by a hedge with a small stream of water running down into the river. Mr Watson grew watercress in the stream and Eileen grew very partial to tongue and watercress sandwiches, made with fresh bread out of the oven and homemade butter. Mr Watkins was a member of Evesham Rowing Club and won many medals. To this day, an oar in Evesham Almonry Museum is a reminder of his prowess as a sculler.

## Chapter Four

# The Thirties and Time for Fishing

Somehow, Ernie found the time to fish and would sit next to the Ferry on the landing stage. His skill as an angler rose ever higher and soon people were asking if they could fish there too. One thing led to another and, before the couple knew it, they were organising fishing contests on the banks of the Avon at Hampton Ferry.

Eileen did the paperwork, booked the contests, and collected the money. Ernie bought a set of Beam scales and, for 3d (12d to a shilling and a shilling is now 5p), he would weigh-in the contest and give the club the results. So, it wasn't long before Evesham became a Mecca for anglers. They would arrive in droves at 8.00 am on Sunday, by train from Birmingham, returning on the 4.50 pm train that night.

And this, of course, brought even more catering opportunities. As the anglers liked to have bacon or sausage sandwiches and a cup of tea when they arrived, Eileen obliged, still serving them out of the small kitchen window at Hampton Ferry House.

She made all her own bread but, reluctant to leave the crusts on a sandwich and equally reluctant to throw the bread away, she started making it into bread pudding to tempt the anglers before they caught the train back. Little did she realise just what an impact this was to have, nor how famous the bread pudding would become. Over the years, many people came just to taste

## Chapter Four

Me with some of Mum's famous bread pudding

and buy it. And Eileen's bread pudding is still on the menu at Hampton Ferry ninety-five years later.

On 10 November 1934, Eileen and Ernie celebrated the arrival of their second child, a boy, Wellesley Gordon Huxley. Things were going exceedingly well, with fishing bringing more people to

Hampton Ferry than they had imagined when they started selling a few fishing permits. Now customers were asking if they could stay the night, so they could fish on Saturday evening plus the whole of Sunday. The only way they could accommodate them was by allowing overnight camping, for which a licence was needed.

Not being quite sure how to do this, Eileen went to visit Squire Rudge, at Abbey Manor to ask him: (a) could they do it and (b) how should they go about it.

To get to the Abbey Manor was a very long walk so Eileen decided to go by boat as far as the Worcester Road and then walk up the hill. The squire was amazed at her ingenuity, so he listened with interest to their plans and gave his blessing to the project. He told Eileen she should apply for the camping licence from Evesham Borough Council, which they swiftly did – receiving the confirmation with delight.

And so, another lucrative scheme was added to the fishing, plants, the punts and the homemade teas. Hampton Ferry Camping site was born, rapidly becoming popular with many anglers camping the night. During the Birmingham and Coventry Industries' holiday fortnight, in the last two weeks in July and the first week in August, there were always huge numbers arriving in Evesham for their holidays. With camping costing 1/6d (seven and a half pence) for a week, whole families descended on the riverside location to enjoy the countryside, the fresh air, the fishing and all the delights the site offered. They brought everything with them, including the kitchen sink – there was even one family which always brought a piano too. And due to this, one of the few rules for the site was: 'No noise or musical instrument after 11.00 pm.'

Those holiday three weeks were the busiest Eileen and Ernie

had ever known. The ferry was in constant use and, once again, Eileen was using her skills in the kitchen to make doughnuts and cocoa to serve on balmy summer evenings. With the catering side growing they jumped at the offer of an old caravan which they gutted to install a sink, a cooker using bottled gas and a counter from where they served bacon and sausage sandwiches with tea or coffee to the fishermen in the morning, bread pudding and tea in the afternoon when the contest was over, and doughnuts and hot cocoa to the campers at night.

The caravan was sited on the opposite side of the river to the house, in a meadow which Ernie had recently acquired from Mr Van der Beken. It happened in this way...

A few weeks earlier, Ernie had been given £5.5s to pay the rent to the Rudge Estate. On his way, he met an old friend who gave him a hot tip for a race that afternoon. Always a bit of a gambler, Ernie put all the rent money on a horse called Raymond. Luckily for him, it romped home at 33–1. Ecstatic, he duly went and paid the rent.

On his way home, he met Mr Van der Beken who was bemoaning the fact that the fire brigade no longer needed to use his meadow for their horses because these had been replaced with automobiles for their fire engines.

Sensing a bargain, Ernie offered to take over the lease on the meadow and this was accepted. So, now he had a meadow where they could have a few more fishing pegs and somewhere to put a caravan, to sell drinks and food. Ernie, therefore, really could not understand why Eileen was not as delighted as he. She was, in fact, furious. What if the horse had not won? What would they have done? How could they have paid the rent? Ernie assured her he knew it would win but, after that, Eileen took care of the money and paid all the bills personally.

But Hampton Ferry was flourishing, with their plants advertised in Exchange & Mart, and much sought after. Almost every day in early spring they would be pulling and packing plants to post off to people to grow in their own gardens. Each afternoon, when everything was packed, Eileen pushed a small flat-bedded wheelbarrow to the Post Office. The sturdy cardboard boxes were in various sizes and with neatly written address labels going all parts of the country. The PO cashier was intrigued and almost disappointed when she found out what the boxes contained.

## Chapter Five

# Family life

Ernie's sisters, Marjorie, Rose, Gwen, Kathleen, Edith, and Barbara, were growing up and soon marrying. Ernie and Eileen did what they could to assist, with Eileen helping with some of the wedding dresses. Ernie gave each of his sisters away and frequently paid for some of the refreshments. Marjorie, the eldest, married John Warnes and moved to Lowestoft; Gwen became Mrs Ludlow and moved to Pershore; Rose married Aubrey Russell and Kathleen David Clarke – remaining in Evesham. Edith married Walter Hiley and moved to Birmingham, and the youngest, Barbara, married Ron Millington and moved to Worcester.

Even when married, they were all frequent visitors to Hampton Ferry. Edith and Walter lived quite a distance away but came most Saturdays staying until Sunday. Walter was 'The man from the Pru' and they enjoyed the journeys in his car. Edith and Eileen were very close, and she was a great help with afternoon teas, served on the riverbank lawn outside the house. Early on Sundays, she would be up to serve tea and sandwiches to the fishermen, and she never minded Walter's fishing trips with Ernie. They had both joined Evesham Jubilee Angling Society and did well in the contests.

In February 1939 Eileen gave birth to her third child Diana Rosalie and this is where I take over my own story.

Three young children, living so close to the river, could have been nerve-wracking for my parents but we were all taught to swim almost before we could walk. A rope, tied to a pole, was joined to a belt that went around the child, who was put into the river. Dad held the pole and each of us would go through the motions of swimming, soon gaining enough confidence to go it alone. Once we could swim across the river unaided, we were promised anything we wanted.

Deirdre asked for and got a tin of condensed milk all to herself. Wellesley asked for a knife to whittle with and then proceeded to test how sharp it was by cutting the ferry rope, earning a severe reprimand. When I made my first successful crossing, I asked for a piano, which duly arrived. Sadly, for me, it was nine-year-old sister. Deirdre who had music lessons, as I was thought too young, at just three and a half. The idea was that Deirdre would then teach me, which didn't happen, but I learned to love music and later tried – and failed – to master the piano.

Dad's method of teaching people to swim was used constantly, and many Scouts earned their swimming badge by the landing stage at Hampton Ferry. Over the years, he must have taught hundreds of children and adults to swim. It was only when he died that we learned he could not swim himself.

As soon as we could swim and hold an oar, we were taught to row a boat, which was on a long rope tied to the landing stage then pushed out into the river for us to row back. Like most children doing something we enjoyed, we learned quickly and all three of us had our own small rowing boats, so did not bother the ferryman when we wanted to cross the river – we just got into our boats and rowed.

Deirdre had already started ballet lessons but, when she was nine, had a very nasty accident and dislocated her hip so severely that, not only her dancing lessons were ended, but she could no longer join Wellesley and me in the things we enjoyed like swimming, rowing and playing on and in the river.

It was the start of several years of pain and hospital appointments for her. Her leg was in a calliper for months and she never fully recovered. Throughout her life, she struggled to bend one leg at the hip, which restricted her activities, but she never complained and remained cheerful and ready to help others.

As Mother was frequently taking Deirdre for hospital treatment Wellesley and I were left to play, spending a lot of our time in the river in the summer. We once had an argument about who could swim the furthest:

'I can swim further than you.'

'No, you can't.'

'Yes, I can.'

Well, there was only one way to settle it so we started swimming, downstream, past the camping site, past Glovers Island, right down to the Black Bridges where the trains crossed the river. There, Wellesley said he'd had enough, pointing out we had to swim back too. So we did and agreed we both could swim a long way if we had to.

By the time we got back to the Ferry mum and dad were frantic looking for us and did not know whether to tell us off or hug us both. In later years, if I was asked what I was good at I would always say swimming. Not fast or anything, but I could swim well.

## Chapter Six

# Additions

Eileen and Ernie were doing very well, with a lot of help from various people, one of whom was little Tommy Pepper. He was only 3 foot 6 inches tall but eager to find work. Soft-hearted Eileen offered him a job on the Ferry as well as helping generally. She fed him and gave him a pay packet each week. He loved this but was a bit unpredictable and it wasn't unusual to find him sleeping under the big elm tree in front of the house. When woken he would jump up and get back to work until tiredness overcame him again. But he was always eager to please and pleasant to have around with his friend Ivy.

She was also short but not as active as Tommy and would spend happy hours doing jigsaw puzzles in the Lounge, where her contribution was to shout out to whoever was doing the Ferry when they had a customer. Ivy would do her puzzles at the three-penny bit table, and, at mealtimes, a cloth was put over the puzzle, the meal eaten, the cloth removed, and puzzle time resumed.

At about this time my dad was given a black and white cross Border Collie/Labrador puppy, a companion for Rocklitz. Toby became a real character at the Ferry, walking the riverbank until selecting one fisherman out of the many, to sit behind. Dad quickly spotted that Toby was sussing out who had meat in their sandwiches. He didn't like cheese, egg, or jam and was usually rewarded for his patience. As Toby grew older, on occasions he would

## Chapter Six

disappear for a week or ten days but always came home. After the initial anxiety, Dad realised he was probably courting a nearby female dog. It was only when Dad went fishing at Offenham, now newly opened to anglers, he discovered Toby's visits were to a golden Labrador at Offenham Ferry. And he had fathered beautiful puppies, certainly, on more than one occasion.

Toby lived until he was twenty-one – a grand age for a dog.

Christmas time was wonderful for us children at Hampton Ferry. On 1 December, Mum would cut up old newspapers in strips, buy small bottles of poster paints and we would sit round the table painting strips of paper to make Christmas decorations, all different colours. The next night we would stick them together (usually with egg white) and we would hang them up decorating all the rooms downstairs ready for Christmas. On Christmas Eve Dad would bring in holly and mistletoe and the house would be decorated in time for Christmas Day.

Of course, it took several evenings to paint enough strips of paper and after Christmas, we would take them all down and burn them on the fire, then toasting bread to have with home-made jam – all part of a lovely Christmastide.

## Chapter Seven

## The War Years

September 1939 and the start of the Second World War brought dramatic change to everyone's lives. Dad was exempt from the 'call-up' being encouraged to plough up his much-loved putting green to 'Dig for Britain'. This was done after a visit from the Man from the Ministry of Agriculture and Fishing (Min of Ag and Fish) who examined the grounds and discussed what he would like to see grown: narcissi, flowering cherry, wallflowers (gillies) orange and burgundy coloured, with some slingets of salad stuff, lettuce, spring onions and radish.

We learned later wallflowers were used to make dye for the khaki for army uniforms. With the flowering cherry trees and narcissi came ten beehives to produce much needed honey. Mum oversaw the hives – Dad would not go anywhere near them if he could help it – and she joined the local beekeepers' association, starting a pastime she enjoyed for the rest of her life.

Just before the war, Dad became interested in pigeons and joined Evesham Racing Pigeon club, little realising how useful this hobby would become. Most mornings he could be seen taking a basket of pigeons, on the front of his bicycle, to Bengeworth Railway Station, ostensibly to train them. It was only much later he revealed some of his birds had been sent to the front line where messages were put in a small thimble on their legs before they flew home. If there was a thimble it would swiftly be removed, put in a small tin, and given to one of us to take to the police station, with instructions to give it to a certain officer. Another of Dad's contributions to the war effort.

So, these were busy years for our parents, with us three children to care for, on top of the work around the Ferry. Then, when the BBC moved to the town bringing many employees needing accommodation, they took in lodgers. There was very little option

Dad with his pigeons

because, if you had room, you were obliged to accommodate a lodger. With three bedrooms, bunk beds were built for Deirdre and Wellesley, while I slept in a drawer, all of us in Mum's and Dad's bedroom, leaving two small bedrooms.

One of our lodgers was Frank Phillips, a newsreader who, in later years, I blamed for my lack of a sense of geography and distance. I had been convinced London was only a few minutes away from our house because he would have breakfast at our house, say: 'I'm off to work!' and within half an hour I heard him on the radio, saying: 'This is Frank Phillips, bringing you the news from London.' So, I reasoned, London could not be very far away.

Billeted with Frank was Thomas Ellin, chief cashier for BBC Lime Grove Studios. Their stay lasted almost six years and we young children were encouraged to call Mr Ellin Uncle Gus – a nickname taken from the Tommy Handley *ITMA (It's That Man Again)* programme in which Gus was the butler. Mr Ellin would make a cup of tea for everyone in the evening, so he was nicknamed Gus the butler and Uncle Gus, which he was called by us children for the rest of his life. He was a legend at the BBC for his scrutiny of expenditure, finding countless ways to save money. When afternoon tea was served by a lady with a trolley, he reduced the range of biscuits to just the Garibaldi, both the least popular and probably the cheapest. Lots were left to be retrieved by Uncle Gus for a later appearance, which caused great hilarity.

Some years later a visitor to Hampton Ferry to see Uncle Gus, recalled being on the beach at Dunkirk and so cold, tired, and hungry he would have given anything for one of those cast-aside Garibaldi biscuits. He thought it ironic to be dreaming only of those biscuits at that stressful time. And the story goes that anyone getting away with padding their expenses used it to call for a celebration. He must have saved the BBC thousands over the years.

As Dad appeared to be relatively well-off, his Uncle Jim also turned up, looking for somewhere to live and work. Mum was not best pleased because Uncle Jim did not wash, constantly smoked a pipe, used foul language and, if he could afford it, was almost permanently drunk.

Worried about his effect on the children, and the pungent smell, she would not have him in the house, so Uncle Jim was given a wooden shed in which to sleep, a bed but no sheets, which he said was 'too posh'. He complained about the food too, calling salad rabbits' grub, bread and jam kids' grub. He wanted steak and eggs which, during and shortly after the war, were hard to come by. As they had chickens and turkeys, eggs were more plentiful, and he did get eggs and bacon. We children would watch him eat fascinated when he picked up an egg with a knife, swallowing it whole. Mum would then have to call us in and talk about our manners.

Old Uncle Jim Huxley was quite a character and became a permanent evening fixture at the Cider Mill pub until closing time, when he went back to his shed. In the winter, he kept the stove going to keep the greenhouse plants safe. He would put in a brick to heat up, then wrapped it in a sack and took to bed to keep his feet warm.

He refused to take out a penny a month insurance to help pay for his funeral, saying: 'One thing for sure is they won't leave me on top, so there is no need to have no fancy insurance.' He did some work on occasion, enjoying chopping wood and sawing logs, for the household fires.

Life at Hampton Ferry was otherwise little changed: people still visited, hiring punts on sunny days, and enjoying afternoon teas. Although food was tightly rationed, huge blocks of sugar were delivered to feed the bees and some was grated for cakes and jams as well as sweeten the teas. As the family had their own chickens and ducks, turkeys and geese, pigs, and a goat, the food supply was plentiful and could be enjoyed by the visitors.

There was also a donkey called Jenny Pearl which we children loved. Mother became interested in breeding rabbits, mostly chinchillas, which were reared and eaten. Their skins were treated so, at Christmas, nearly all the presents for friends and relations were either warm gloves or hats of the beautiful grey fur, all made by Mum who grew increasingly clever with her needle.

Dad made a huge contribution too. We had wonderful vegetables from the garden, plus strawberries, gooseberries, raspberries, black and red currants and a few apple and plum trees. We always had fruit even if it had been bottled months earlier.

Each spring Dinah the turkey and her mate Charlie would produce fertile eggs and the resulting chicks, named Jim, Rose, Pat etc after Dad's brothers and sisters, were given to them for Christmas dinner. The turkeys also proved to be the best guards you could have. If anyone came near the Ferry they made terrible squawking sounds, warning the ferryman of customers.

One day a black Labrador dog chased the turkeys into the river. Panic-stricken, Dad called us kids to get into our boats but there was no need: they swam down river in single file to the ferry steps, climbed out and headed back to dry land.

Luckily, we escaped most of the atrocities of war, but a bomb did fall in the river not far from the house, blowing out the windows. It was meant for the railway bridges, known as the Black Bridges, about a mile or so downstream. Fortunately, it missed, and our house was soon repaired.

During the early years our mother had asked Cadbury's if she could buy chocolate direct from them to sell. Her order had to be big to make it worth them delivering but, for many years, a direct order was made twice a year. Chocolate was rationed and could only be bought with government sweet coupons, which increased the value of her order, so it was locked in a huge, tall cupboard in a recess in the small dining room, but the tempting smell of chocolate gave it away. Only Mum had the key, but Wellesley proved adept at opening the cupboard with his multi-gadget Scout knife. Then, he would carefully open and unwrap a bar and fold it all back and replace it – but with nothing inside. He was quickly found out and his little tricks were stopped. When he grew older, he often wondered whether he should just have eaten the chocolate and not tried to be clever by replacing the wrapper. We will never know.

## Chapter Eight
## War-Time Guests and an Artist

Hampton Ferry was a hive of activity, with more work than could be done by one man so Dad asked for and got help, in the shape of German prisoners of war. They were interned at Littleton, near Evesham and brought to the Ferry each day.

By now our parents had increased their land and leased another eleven acres downstream from the Ferry. They had also bought Mr Watson's bungalow and planted asparagus on a large portion of the ground. There was also the land known as Glovers Island and past that, was the newly leased land, which became known as Paradise. Most Sunday evenings Dad would take the dogs for a walk and say to Mum: 'I am going to view the estate', always saying on his return: 'I have just been to Paradise, it is so peaceful and quiet down there I love it.' From then on it was always known by us all as Paradise.

Four German prisoners were allotted to us: Hans, Albert, Rudi, and Fritz, all of whom were extremely good workers, being either land workers or farm owners in their home country. They quickly tidied up the land and the crops flourished with their care. Mum made sure they were fed and treated well, so friendships were formed that lasted a lifetime.

One Christmas, Albert made all the family a pair of slippers each, beautifully woven and plaited out of string. They were a real work of art. He cried when Mum gave him a Christmas jumper that she had knitted for him, because it reminded him so much of his family in Germany and of what he was missing. Such is the travesty of war.

Their value was to show up even more one sunny day when two couples were out in a punt and messing about on the river. Inevitably, one of the girls fell in, but Rudi, who was working on the newly planted asparagus beds, raced down, dived in and saved her from drowning. This act of bravery led to his release and a return home to Germany, but he burst into tears when he heard, saying he did not want to go back because, as an officer who'd been captured, he knew he would be sent to Siberia. He promised to write to Mum and let her know his fate, but we never heard from him again.

During the evacuation at Dunkirk, many soldiers were returned to England and put on trains to anywhere they could be looked after, fed, and watered. Hampton Ferry was one such place. A railway line ran immediately behind the Ferry House, directly from Evesham to Ashchurch and then south.

A train unloaded about twenty soldiers plus tents and some equipment into the care of local people. Our parents quickly made soup, bread, and meals for them. The soldiers had all been so grateful Mum was surprised about three days later to find one crying. Thinking he was ill she asked what was wrong.

When he replied, she felt silly for not thinking of it before. Although he was home in England, his family probably thought he was dead because he had no money or means of writing or phoning to say he was back safe in England. The next telephone bill Mum and Dad had was by far the highest ever, but they made no complaints. They also bought stamps and provided notepaper for the soon much happier soldiers. They were not to stay long however, as they were soon taken to barracks once the Dunkirk evacuation was completed.

During the soldiers' stay at Hampton Ferry, the pleasure boat that still went up and down the river Avon, somehow caught its propeller on the Ferry rope. Very anxious not to add the cost of a new rope as well as the difficulty in obtaining one, Dad asked for help. Two soldiers, who were good swimmers, dived in to free it. Grateful as always, Mum gave them twelve chocolate biscuits each, a real luxury and one of them signed Deirdre's autograph book, with the comment 'All for a dozen chocolate biscuits.'

The camping site prospered and did a good trade, and an artist called Mr Pegram started selling caricatures to some of the visitors. His week's rent for one tent was 1/6d so every week Mr Pegram gave Dad a 2/- piece and told him to keep the change, so he became a much-valued customer. For several years running, he would come in May and stay through the summer sometimes not going home until late October or early November.

It was usual for Dad to go fishing almost every Thursday, sometimes taken by another keen fisherman in his car, who was then Evesham's Chief Police Constable. But, one Thursday, when the Chief Constable arrived, he rather shamefacedly refused the usual offer of a cup of tea, saying he was sorry, but he was there on official business. Dad wondered what he could possibly have done to bring the police to his door but soon learned that they were investigating counterfeit money that was circulating in Evesham, in the form of 2/- pieces. One had been spotted being banked almost every week by Mr E W Huxley and it didn't take Dad long trace it back to Mr Pegram.

So, when asked if he knew where it came from, he had to admit reluctantly he thought he did but could not believe it.

When the police examined Mr Pegram's sturdy double bell tent, they found a very tidy and clean bed, some clothes neatly folded and kept in an upturned orange box and another small box, with kitchen pot, knife, fork and spoon, mug, and a plate, all tidily laid out. The pot-bellied stove stood proudly in the middle, with a chimney going up and out through the tent next to the tent pole. On top of the stove were two metal plates, the size of a dinner plate, with dyes of 2/- pieces – one plate for one side of the coin and the other for the other side. Mr Pegram, a clever artist, had found a way to double or treble his money.

All English coins, pre-1947, were made of solid silver. So Mr Pegram would melt some lead and place it between the dyes and, when solid and cold, cover them with silver from melted real coins. No wonder he could tip well. Many years later, when I visited Hindlip, the Police Headquarters and museum, I was amazed to see the dyes and a storyboard telling of the forger found at Hampton Ferry, who had been sent to prison for some considerable time for his artistic efforts. Several years later, when that museum closed, these artefacts were acquired by the Evesham Historical Society and are now an exhibit in the Almonry Heritage Centre Evesham. Pictures and the pots and dyes are all still on show to-day.

## Chapter Nine
## Peace and the 1947 Floods

Peace was declared, the war was over, but nothing would ever be quite the same again. Women had become accustomed to working in factories, earning their own money, and doing a responsible job. But the returning soldiers expected to carry on as before so there were many hard re-adjustments to be made.

But our family was doing well. Everyone worked hard and was rewarded with a very pleasant lifestyle. We children were now all at school. Deirdre and Wellesley had started at Hampton School and later moved to Greenhill School, where I joined them when I was four, all riding to school on our bicycles. We even enjoyed the severe winter of 1947 when the river froze and for several weeks, we could walk on the ice to cross the river.

When the thaw started, Dad got us out of bed early one morning to watch the ice break up. The river at Abbey Park is only about three to four feet deep and the ice there melted first and started flowing downstream. These huge lumps of ice slid under the ice on the lower reaches and, as it got to Hampton Ferry, made an intense noise as the ice cracked into a million pieces, sounding like a shattered windscreen would to-day. There was a huge eruption as the ice broke with some flying up into the air. In hardly any time at all the river was in flood.

I stood on the riverbank and cried as I watched my small clinker-built boat smash into a thousand pieces like matchwood. At the start of the freeze, Dad had taken the other boats out of the river, leaving just the one he thought was strong enough to withstand the pressure of freezing water. My boat was soon replaced and, to my delight, was even bigger than the old one.

When the floods came, Wellesley and I were in our element. As the river rose, it brought wood and tree trunks floating down stream. We would get into Wellesley's boat, and he would row

A harsh winter on the Avon

while I held a rope with a loop on one end, like a lassoo. Dad would be on the bank holding the other end of the rope. When we got near enough to any wood it was lassoed and Dad would pull it ashore. He always said that wood kept him warm three times: once when he pulled it out of the river, the second time when he chopped it up and the third time when it was burning in the fireplace.

The year 1947 saw, perhaps, the quickest thaw on record and in a very short space of time the river Avon was a raging torrent, with the highest recorded flood of 12' 6" which was fascinating to watch and enjoyed particularly by Wellesley and me as we rowed over the river to get to school. Rowing upstream from the house to Cooks bend, we hit the current at its strongest which took us over the river to the quiet waters which were covering all the fields across the Corporation Meadow, Staites Nurseries and the cricket pitch at Evesham Sports Ground. Then we were on to the rugby pitch where we would tie the boat up to the gate in the far corner, walk up on to the bridges and not far to school – just up Greenhill from the railway station. Coming home, we did everything in reverse, rowed on the quiet waters all the way up to Cooks Bend and then hit the current. Dad would be waiting with a long punting boat hook for me to catch as Wellesley rowed by and we would then be pulled into the quieter waters by the house and safely home. I was eight at the time and Wellesley was eleven. I have three grown up sons now and I would be terrified if they ever tried to do this.

The floods filled the Ferry House cellar with water and, when the river dropped back to normal, it was full of trapped fish. We were told to put on our bathing costumes . . . in March. Dad filled dustbins with water, Wellesley and I paddled about in the cellar with landing nets, catching the fish, which Dad put in the bins and then returned to the river. We were very cold but had really enjoyed it, catching the most fish in the easiest possible way. An eel was the last fish we managed to catch and took some considerable time for it to be returned to the river.

Over the years many strange things floated down the river but perhaps the strangest was a chicken coop, complete with chickens sitting on the roof. Wellesley and I were immediately dispatched to go and capture them. It took some doing and some considerable time but eventually the coup and the chickens were rescued. Very much aware that, if left with no fencing around them, the fox would get them, Wellesley and Dad got to work to put up chicken wire to make a safe enclosure and the chickens seemed quite happy with plenty of grass and gravel to peck at.

Later that evening Dad went out to shut them in, only to find, to his amazement, they were all sitting neatly on top of the chicken wire around their enclosure. They jumped or flew down into the coop so Dad could shut the door. They could have easily got out of their run but never did. The local newspaper reported how they had been found but, as no one claimed them, there were a dozen more laying chickens which helped feed the family quite some time.

## Chapter Ten

## Business is Growing

Mr Watkins, our next-door neighbour had died, and our parents had bought his wooden bungalow to make into a café for the fishermen and campers. The menu by now included eggs on toast and a proper breakfast of bacon, beans, sausage and egg with tea or coffee. Mum wanted to branch out and sell a greater variety of food, which meant buying a large ice-cream fridge, with two compartments and lids that lifted off to access the contents. It was bought directly from Frigidaire and delivered in a big wooden box. Once off the lorry, it was obvious it was too big to put on the Ferry to cross the river until it was unpacked from its box, when it just squeezed on. Many years later a magazine was sent to us from Canada with a picture of the ice-cream fridge on the Ferry, in an advertisement 'Frigidaire – We deliver anywhere.' We still don't know who took that photograph.

After the war Mum kept her bees and was frequently asked to take a swarm if it was in garden or another inconvenient place. She had passed her driving test, after five attempts, and had bought a second-hand car from her brother-in-law Ron. So now she could do the heavy shopping by car rather than bicycle. It also came in useful when she went to take a swarm of bees – not many people who would be happy to have an Ali Baba basket in the back of their car filled with bees, but she was never concerned and, more importantly, never got stung.

## Chapter Ten

Dad, of course, steered clear and would have nothing to do with them, except eat their honey. He also never ever learned to drive a car or even the tractor. He was a clever man, if not academic. His day off was always a Thursday when he would go fishing. He fished pretty well all the rivers in the Midlands and South of England and was frequently taken out by other fishermen who considered it a privilege to drive him there and back. Some came from quite a distance to pick him up to go fishing and bring him back before going home.

Dad loved going to some of the auctions held weekly at the Smithfield Market and whenever there was a Ministry of Defence Auction he would go. He was interested in one of the small boats – Army pontoons – they had listed that needed an outboard motor. He thought it would be useful when clearing the fishing pegs etc. so off he went and, yes, bought a pontoon but, one day in the early 1950s, he came home and told Mum he had bought a new café because the caravan was not really big enough. Oh, and he'd got tables and chairs too. Mum could not believe him but, sure enough, he had bought a brand-new pigsty from Wigfield and Pluck which was 16 ft x 24 ft but only four foot high.

When Mum told him this would not be worth bothering with as there weren't enough pygmies in Evesham to warrant such a low building, Dad said he planned to build bricks up to five foot and put the wooden bit on top, giving plenty of headroom. With planning permission obtained, work commenced and everyone was involved. The footings had to be dug out, then cement laid. Albert was a willing digger, and I pushed the wheelbarrow with the surplus soil, moving it nearer the riverbank to make some of the fishing pegs easier to get to. Then water had to be connected and electricity but soon Mum was looking for crockery and cutlery, a cooker, fridge, catering chip pan, a water boiler to make tea and another to wash up.

One of the things Mum wasn't happy about was the cement floor. She wanted to put down lino or floor covering but finances didn't run to it. But Mum, being determined she wasn't having a dull grey cement floor, bought some liquid lino and painted the floor in green and cream squares, which looked really good. There

Uncle Albert and Auntie Gladys with Ernest and Eileen Huxley outside the new cafe built from a pigpen on bricks.

were pretty green and cream curtains with a hunting scene on, that Mum had made from material bought at Birmingham Rag Market, and the four wooden tables and sixteen chairs that Dad had bought at the auction were sanded and stained, so it really did look very nice.

There was a narrower door behind the counter for us to get the groceries brought in ready for baking and at the other end

## Chapter Ten

was the entrance to the cafe through big double sliding doors. It was a huge success and, as we frequently had 150 to 175 anglers fishing the weekend contests, it meant the first sixteen could sit down and eat a breakfast. After a very short time bench seats were made and fixed to the wall so more could sit down if it was raining or very windy and cold.

So Mum had gone from serving teas out of the kitchen in the house, to a caravan opposite the house where just sandwiches and tea/coffee were served – which Mum had nicknamed the 'Interval' – and now she had the café, which she called 'Bright Interval' where she hoped they would serve proper meals.

The fishing was doing very well, mostly because there were only three fisheries that could cater for so many anglers: Kidderminster AA, Worcester AA and Evesham Town and Hampton Ferry Waters.

Evesham being on the Warwickshire Avon was always a sell-out when the River Severn was in flood but was quite busy most of the time anyway.

## Chapter Eleven
# Growing Up – Deirdre and Wellesley

Every Sunday morning all three of us went to Sunday School at the Methodist Church at the bottom of Bridge Street. Our Dad only went to church for weddings, christenings, and funerals, and even then, reluctantly. Our Mother felt it was important we had some religious education and made sure we went, although she also rarely went to church. Sundays were always busy days for her, but it did not stop her from being very Christian in the way she lived. She had compassion and love for almost every living thing, a strong sense of right and wrong and a great sense of humour.

The Methodist Church started a youth club which Deirdre and Wellesley thoroughly enjoyed. They went two evenings a week to play table tennis, football, netball, darts and meet other children to play games with and generally have fun.

In 1948, two members, who played in Evesham Town Band, were asked if they would like some old brass instruments, found in Mickleton Village Hall. Mick Sharp and John Turvey jumped at the opportunity, repairing, cleaning and making them shine – the start of Avonbank Brass Band.

Soon people were asking to join and, by 1950, Deirdre, Wellesley and I all joined. Deirdre learnt to play the cornet, continuing for many years until she married and had children. Wellesley was taught to play the trombone but, in less than a year, his love of rowing proved the greater, and he left to join Evesham Rowing Club as rowing and the river was more his sport.

When I was just eleven, I joined too, playing a cornet, then tenor horn and then a baritone, then back to a tenor horn, which I continued (with a few breaks to get married and have children) until the early 1970s. Our parents must have been very understanding with three children all learning brass instruments at the same time. How lucky there were no close neighbours!

Avonbank Brass Band had a strong female element. I'm far right and Deirdre is next to me.

We were all growing up now and Deirdre had the only boyfriend she ever had – Bob Turvey – they met through the Methodist Church. He was soon a regular visitor to Hampton Ferry and, when Bob escorted Deirdre home, Dad would be waiting to make sure they did not take too long saying good night. Deirdre and I shared a bedroom, and she would always go up to her bedroom, open the window and talk to Bob, and on occasions he would sing to her. I thought this the most romantic thing I had seen and enjoyed it as much as Deirdre did.

When they were courting a wonderful Mr Warren, who ran the youth club, did much to keep young people on the right track including Bob. He and Deirdre became youth club leaders and Bob was also a lay preacher in his early 20s and very involved with the Methodist church.

They did not have any children at first so they both decided they would like to foster children, which they did for several years and were both great parents helping a lot of children who needed some love and care. They then had two children of their own, David and Stephen and proved yet again that they were wonderful parents.

Obviously they grew out of the Youth Club as such, but as they got older they organised 'Open House' on a Friday evening for older people, to meet and make friends and it was not long before they decided to try and purchase a mini bus so they could take people out for a day trip or an afternoon trip. Somehow, they raised enough funds and Bob would drive the minibus and Deirdre would organise who and where they would go. This proved a great service to some of the elderly in Evesham and it was also used on Sundays to fetch people from their homes and take them to Church. This worked for several years until Bob was unable to drive any more, they had another volunteer who did some of the driving, but this did not last.

When Bob died my family said we would try and organise the minibus ourselves, which we did for a year or two, and hired the minibus out to local charities, for which they paid a small fee but as these charities were getting involved with fund-raising, some of them bought their own. Sadly we had to admit defeat and had to sell it. Deirdre and Bob had done a really fantastic job but we could not get the necessary driving volunteers to do the work they had both done, organising and driving. Open House was still going and when we sold the minibus we gave them the money.

Deirdre died the day before her seventieth birthday. She had cancer. She was treated and was in remission, but she had to go to Cheltenham Hospital every six months for a check-up. On occasions I used to take her, and we'd make a day out of it. The last time we were to go, it was a lovely day, and she was full of beans as she went in to see the specialist. However, when she came out, she looked as if she had aged ten years. He'd told her the cancer had come back. She said she couldn't face having anymore treatment and he said, in that case, he would do the best he could for her for a few years – in fact she lived for a further four years until 2003. A great loss which left a big gap in the family.

Wellesley had been sent to boarding school in the Cotswolds and he hated it. He came home sometimes at weekends, and, with rationing still in place, school meals consisted mostly of potatoes, bread to fill up the youngsters. So, he came home considerably fatter and heavier than he had been when he started at Hill Place School. Mum was horrified and I had missed my brother too so his stay at a boarding school only lasted a few terms, then he went to Blackminster School. Riding his bike to and from school soon got his weight back to normal for a fourteen-year-old boy.

When he left school, he worked for Dad in the market garden, he did not enjoy it because it did not teach him what he really wanted to learn, like how to strip down a tractor or a motor car.

He did not read much and was definitely a country boy. A keen fisherman like Dad, they spent many happy hours together on the riverbank.

On one occasion, Wellesley was at the bar with his crew for a rowing club dinner and they were talking among themselves as men do. One of them announced: 'I bet any of you a pint who goes up and kisses the next female who comes through that door.' Well, the next person was me! My brother came up to me and said: 'Please don't squeal or shout just give me a kiss! And of course, I did – he was my brother. They all clapped and cheered at the bar which I thought was strange. Later I found out what it was and asked what they'd expected to happen – they thought it would be a slapped face. I was nearly 15 at the time: Wellesley was almost three years older than me.

As time went by it became obvious that Wellesley was much happier sitting on a tractor or a machine of almost any sort rather than using a fork or hoe to till the ground. So, he established himself doing what he liked best, riding the tractor and ploughing, mowing, spraying, scuffling etc for other market gardeners who did not have tractors of their own.

Many of us have heard of the barter system but Wellesley used it to perfection. If a customer could not afford to pay him cash, they paid him in kind whatever it might be, and he would then either exchange it for something he wanted or would sell it on to someone else.

Mum and Dad would say where do you get your money from, where did you get that or this from? For example, he fished a lot – a net of sprouts was worth three pints of maggots and he had an orchard at the top of Clark's Hill up Red Lane, with a shed where he kept his tractor in. He picked cowslips, damsons, dandelion, he would make wine and all the neighbours up there would say: 'We're going to the club and enjoy the wine.' Our parents had no idea how he made any money, but he always paid his bills and got on rather well.

Wellesley had a girlfriend called Daphne. She lived in the Cotswolds and there was a bus into Evesham twice a week, which was not convenient if you wanted to work. Daphne worked in the sweet shop on Merstow Green every Saturday. She was introduced to the family and got on quite well with all of us.

When Daphne left school, it was very difficult for her to find work in the village where she lived, so Wellesley asked Mum and Dad if they could find any work for her, and could she come and live with us. Mum spoke to Daphne's mother, and it was arranged between them that they would give it a try. Sadly, Wellesley and Daphne's courtship did not survive living so closely together but Daphne worked and lived with us until she got married several years later to David Haywood and was close to our family for the rest of her life.

Their daughter Clare is still close to our family, and we see her regularly. She has always treated my sons like she would a cousin and as teenagers frequently went out with other friends, as John had a car and did not drink, drove them all to the discos and clubs in Worcester at weekends.

When Wellesley was eighteen, he was called up to do his National Service, and most of it he enjoyed because he was in motor maintenance during his two years and they taught him how to strip a vehicle down properly, he was in his element. Now, when Wellesley was about ten his grandmother on his mother's side had heard him swearing, which did not go down well. She washed his mouth out with carbolic soap and he never let any of the family hear him swear again. It was never mentioned again until he was in the Army and sent to Korea as an MT Driver. He sent a postcard home which said simply: 'Grandma would have a full-time job with her carbolic soap if she was on board this ship.' It made our parents smile.

He spent almost two years in Korea and was in a NAAFI one time, waiting for the officer he was driving to finish at a meeting. He got talking to one of the other drivers and asked where each other came from. Wellesley said the Midlands, the other guy said be more specific and he replied: 'A small town you will never have heard of . . . Evesham.' There was a hearty chuckle and he said: 'I come from an even smaller town but guess you will have heard of it. I come from Pershore.'

They started talking of the folks back home and were surprised how many they both knew and then he asked: 'Are you any relation to the Huxley that owns Hampton Ferry?' He said: 'Yes, that is my dad.' The response was: 'What in the hell are you doing in the Army, surely your dad could have bought you out with all the Huxley millions.' Wellesley was amazed and in his next letter home he asked why he had not been bought out of the Army when they had so much money. Mum replied as she always did with a quick remark: 'They have got it wrong – the Huxley millions is not in money but in kids, with ten brothers and sisters Ernie had lost count of the nieces and nephews.' As Deirdre was to find out years later when tracing the family tree, yes, there were seemingly millions of Huxleys.

Wellesley met and married Maureen, who came from

Wednesbury and came to Evesham on her holidays. They had a lovely wedding and lived in Church Road, Hampton for several years and then bought a house on Peewit Road. He carried on his business, working round and about with three greenhouses as well as his tractor. They had two children Nicholas and Andrea.

He sadly died aged fifty-two, in 1986. He had had diabetes and collapsed in the New Year. He was taken to Worcester Royal where they'd operated and put a stent in. I took Maureen to see him, and he sat up in bed, saying he was feeling better than he had for years. As she was talking to him, feeling hugely relieved, there was a minor commotion as doctors and nurses came running in and Maureen was asked to leave. And he died. They had been monitoring his condition remotely and had seen the sudden turn for the worse.

On the following day we had to register his death in Worcester Registry Office and, while we sat in the waiting room, we had to sit through two weddings. We were terribly upset to be in one big room with people coming in for happy occasion while we were mourning our loss. We did comment on it afterwards and I think the waiting room has been changed now.

He died in January and in the April, there was a knock at the door and a man asked for Wellesley. I said: 'Well, I know where he is, but you can't see him because I'm sorry to tell you he has died.' He said: 'Well, what am I going to do with these?' He had two tiny lambs on a string and said: 'Here you'd better have them.' Wellesley had done some work for him the previous year been promised the first two lambs in return, so I took them in, which Maureen then sold on.

After he died, Maureen had to go to the bank. He'd always

paid everything – mortgage, insurance, rates, gas, electricity and so on, giving her the housekeeping money each week. I went with her to the NatWest, where the manager was Bob Turner. He said Wellesley had always fascinated him as he always kept just £5 in the bank – never less. If he paid in £10 2/6 it meant he had written a cheque for £10 2/6. Then, one day he came in and asked for the money to buy a new tractor.

There was no way the bank could give him a loan on what he had in his account, but Wellesley explained about the Evesham Custom which, up until then, Bob hadn't heard much of.

This briefly says: A landlord allows his tenant undisturbed occupation, subject to the land being properly managed and the rent regularly paid; A tenant may improve his holding, for example by planting fruit trees or building a shed, without obtaining permission from his landlord; A tenant who wishes to give up his tenancy is able to introduce a new tenant to the landlord with the amount of compensation, known as ingoing, being agreed between the outgoing and incoming persons; If the landlord has good reason for not accepting the prospective new tenant, he must then personally compensate the old one, so that the latter is no worse off financially for improvements he may have made,

The orchard on his land had fruit trees, so the bank agreed to give the loan and he faithfully repaid it. Most of the land around here is owned by the Rudge estate and Wellesley had a lease for several acres of fruit trees at the top of Clarkes hill.

Harvesting the fruit was always done for Wellesley by a family of gypsies. Granny Smith had four sons who were all married and had several children. They all worked. The men climbed ladders, the women picked what they could reach, and the children picked

## Chapter Eleven

up off the floor. Wellesley was quite often amazed that they all turned up because he never contacted them but, just as the season started, they turned up year after year.

Granny Smith always dealt with the money side of things. Wellesley would go and speak to her when they arrived, and they would agree a price which would duly be paid. He would settle the money by visiting her caravan where he was always impressed at how beautiful it was and by how much lovely crystal glassware she had. It seemed incredible to think of such fragile glass travelling around the country in a caravan.

Wellesley had a contract with a canning firm, and they would contact him and say they wanted so many chips of plums by twelve noon or damsons or apples, which ever they were picking. The family came every year to that part of Hampton and would pick for whoever owned the fruit. They would bring their caravans and stay in the orchard. The women would do the shopping and Granny Smith ruled them all with a rod of iron. She decided what they should eat, and oversee the cooking. Meat was put on a spit and a fire lit and the meat would cook. Bread or rolls would have been bought and, when dinner was ready, Granny would cut off a piece of meat for each family, the size of the meat depended on the size of the family. They would all sit round and literally pull the meat apart, break the bread and eat. Wellesley had great trouble teaching his two children that this was not the way you ate, you sat at the table and cut your food with a knife and fork.

## Chapter Twelve

## My Dreams and the Reality

As for me, well, one has one's dreams and I never achieved any of them. My future had better things in store. When I joined Avonbank Brass Band I was eleven and I loved music. I did not have a natural talent, so I worked hard at doing it. I had also always wanted to travel and see the world, so I made up my mind, at about fourteen or fifteen that, when I left school, I would join the Women's Royal Air Force Band so I would travel, and I would be doing everything I wanted to.

I was fortunate that the National Youth Brass Band had been holding residential tuition schools since 1947, and I applied to join. A lot depended on what instruments you played and there were lots who played cornets and tenor horns so that's when I switched to baritone because that's what they wanted. We went twice a year in the Spring and Autumn half terms.

The first time I went I was fourteen. There were 108 children, all under sixteen and only eight were girls. So, we had a ball. We stayed for a week, and they had hired a whole school. In the morning in your group, according to the instrument you played, you had instruction. After lunch we had band practice and played all together – a wonderful experience.

Later that year I went to the Autumn School when Sir Malcolm Sargent was the conductor. I'll never forget it. We were all in the hall tuning up and the noise was incredible – everyone was blowing their instrument, blowing, or playing up and down the scales. Then Sir Malcolm Sargent walked in, up to the podium and tapped with his baton. Instantly it was like turning the sound off. It was totally silent, when before, the noise had been horrendous.

He said: 'Ladies and gentlemen: the Queen.' Now we were all under sixteen and we'd never been addressed as ladies and gentlemen before, but we'd all been taught how to play the national anthem. After the first note there was a visible gasp because we couldn't believe what we'd heard. It was the first time we'd played with such a big band. It was wonderful.

He was brilliant with young people. I must confess that first band practice he frightened the living daylights out of most of us. We were playing something, and he stopped, pointed to someone and said: 'I'm sorry that's B flat you should be playing.' We were all terrified of playing the wrong note. Out of a hundred of us! How did he hear that? How did he know who it was! My guess was that he didn't. but it certainly kept all of us on our toes. I can't remember what music we played but we played all week and on Friday we were to do a recording for television, so we went to the studios and played. It was big, with technicians and cameras all over the place. Sir Malcolm Sergeant told us we were giving a half hour concert of the music we had been playing and rehearsing all week. There would be no stops and starts, we'd go right through. When we finished, we had to put our instruments on our laps and hold them without moving for two minutes, because that's when the credits would roll. Now two minutes is a long time but then it ended, and Sir Malcolm Sargent said: 'Thank you very much, ladies and gentlemen.'

The technicians and all the people there clapped and when

they stopped, Sir Malcolm Sargent told us: 'Ladies and gentlemen, I can't impress enough to you how unusual it is for the staff and cameramen to clap.

'Last week they pre-recorded Shirley Bassey and they didn't clap her.' They had been impressed by what we'd done as kids, and we were only kids, some not yet in their teens.

Sir Adrian Boult was the conductor one time and one of these weeks, I heard the expression: 'Once a Bandsman – Always a Bandsman.' How true that has proved to be for me. I am President of Avonbank Brass Band where, for me, it all started.

And I am now also president of Wychavon Festival of Brass and have been involved since its inception in 1990. Roger Spragg had worked so hard to establish the Brass Band Festival that, on his death, I was honoured to be asked to be their President.

Brass bands come from all over the country and there are five sections, from Championship to Fourth section, all doing a concert-contest. Each band has twenty minutes to put on a concert and we allow thirty minutes in all, getting on and off the stage. It's now held every year in the autumn in Evesham. To spend all day listening to wonderful concerts is a bandsman's dream.

But I owed my brass band career to a bit of luck as Mum and Dad only let me go to play in the Avonbank band because Deirdre was in it, and I could go there and back with her. There was another boy in the band called Albert so Deirdre and her boyfriend Bob asked if he would walk home with me so they could be on their own. I was eleven and he was fourteen but, from that walking home, we went out until I was eighteen and it was a romance.

I'd left school at fifteen, as you did then, and I'd been helping the family business while my mother went into hospital for an operation. We had the caravan on the Evesham side of the river where we did tea and coffee and bacon sandwiches, on the meadow where the firemen used to keep their horses. We also did hot chocolate and doughnuts that mum had made. So I started off there and I've never really left although, at that time I kept thinking, wait until I was eighteen.

In the summer we were busy but in the winter we weren't. My Dad knew everybody, I don't know how because he never went anywhere, other than fishing. He had been talking to the man in charge of Smithfield market at the top of the High Street, who said one of his girls had gone on maternity leave and needed temporary help. My Dad said I was good on the phone and could write, so I worked there for about four months during the winter and thoroughly enjoyed it. I'd go round when they were auctioning the stock and note what it was and how much it had fetched. When I left, one of the growers said: 'We're sorry to see you go. We've been dealing with this market for years and it's the only time we've ever been able to read what we've sold'; one bought me a bunch of flowers, another a pot plant and others some chocolate. I couldn't believe it.

From there I went to Black and White garages for A. .E Marsh in Harvington, for six to eight months then to the coal merchant in High Street Evesham and from there I got a regular job at the Evesham Telephone Exchange. No more temping for me,

By then I was more involved with the band. Albert went off to do his National Service and had said that, if we got married, he'd have a marriage allowance, but Dad said: 'Not until you are twenty-one.' He'd said the same to Deirdre, who had wanted to marry at eighteen or nineteen.

Now, we used to have different Ferry boys. Mum and Dad had found out the hard way that if you employed one person and they were ill or on holiday you had to do it all yourself. The Ferry ran for twelve hours a day, seven days a week, so they employed twenty-eight boys who all did one three-hour shift, or two, if one was ill or on holiday. They were all thirteen to fourteen years old and delighted to have a little extra pocket money. I think over the years, most of the boys in Hampton had been a Ferry boy.

One, Terry, had had rickets as a child so was never sporty, but very good with a pen and at English. He became a trainee reporter at the *Journal* and was doing very well. When he was about sixteen or seventeen there was big homosexual scandal in Evesham – this was in the late '40s and '50s, when it was illegal. I'd never heard of it. Some of them involved were prominent people in the town.

Terry did not have a very happy home life and my mother literally mothered him. One day he came and said: 'I'm going to have to upset you. I don't want you to be cross, but I've got to tell you. Next week I'm going to court.' He was involved in the proceedings.

My Mum really didn't believe it until she had to, but she wouldn't accept he was an instigator, rather that he was a victim. He was a pretty boy, yes but much younger than all the others involved. My father had absolutely no patience with that kind of thing or anyone like that. Didn't talk about. Didn't do it. Ignore it and it would go away. But my mum wouldn't have it and she said it was going to ruin Terry's life. So, she went round Hampton and got lots of signatures from people saying he was an upstanding young man and not a criminal.

On the due day, she went to court to speak on his behalf. Dad was furious. The magistrate asked where she'd got the signatures and she said: 'I went round Hampton and knocked on doors.' And the upshot was that Terry's case was not dismissed but, if he joined the Army and went and did his National Service there would be no further action. He was coming up to eighteen so he went and did his National Service. He did not think they would accept him because he'd had rickets as a child, but they did. He was doubly grateful to my mum, writing to her twice a week at least.

He'd already done shorthand and typing coming out top of his class. There was a job in Fontainebleau in France, at the NATO headquarters, and they asked him if he'd like to go there, because they really didn't want him in the Army because of his feet. Off he went to Fontainebleau.

This was when petrol and fuel were rationed and hard to get, so you couldn't travel where you wanted because you couldn't get the coupons. Terry knew my Mum wanted to travel as much as me but, as Dad never wanted to leave the county, never mind the country foreign holidays weren't on the cards for her.

He wrote to Mum and told her, if we came over by car, he could get the petrol coupons. A lot of the soldiers bought cars while stationed in France because they were given a petrol allowance and so got coupons. Terry had always been cinema mad, loved Hollywood and his dream had been to go to the Cannes film festival. Now he was in France and suggested Mum brought the car over and we could go to Cannes on holiday.

I was delighted and so was Mum. But Albert and I fell out over it. He said: 'I thought we were saving up to get married not go gallivanting abroad.' I honestly thought, after the holiday when I came back, we'd make it up.

## Chapter Thirteen
# A French Adventure and a Pair of Gloves

Terry said one of his mates called Jock was coming with us – I'd assumed he was homosexual. I was just eighteen and learning to drive, so off we went to Dover to catch the ferry. The car park was empty, as one boat had just loaded up and we were an hour early for the next. But the crew asked if we wanted to catch the boat that was due to leave, even though they'd taken up the gangplank, so we had to drive across on two planks. My Mum said she wasn't driving over them but, with the arrogance of youth, I told her to move over, I would drive, and I did.

We had to drive through Paris to get to Fontainebleau, and, as I was going round the Arch de Triumph, we got a flat tyre. What a place to pick but I got out of the car and being only eighteen and considerably slimmer than now, was soon surrounded by eight or nine gendarmes, who changed the wheel and put on the spare. So we carried on to Fontainebleau, arriving about 7pm much later than anticipated.

Terry had told us we couldn't miss the big golden gates at the entrance – but he failed to tell us there were at least ten of them. Each member of NATO had one. The first was French who told us to go to the next, which was Italian. The next one was American where we were greeted with: 'Gee it's great to meet someone who speaks English.' And they got two motorbikes to escort us round to the British barracks.

## Chapter Thirteen

We said we'd come to see Corporal White and were told he'd gone on holiday. We said we knew that as we'd come to pick them up to go to the South of France. They'd apparently left that afternoon about 4.00 pm so the military police were sent to find them – and they were in a pub. They were normally paid 14/6 a week but a £1 a day subsistence when they were on leave and stayed in the country rather than be flown home, which was how they knew they could afford the holiday, especially as we'd brought the vehicle and they had already bought the petrol coupons.

We went into somewhere to wait, and one soldier asked if we would like a cup of tea. By this time, we were ready to kill for a cuppa and looked hopefully at the big urn. It had a tiny gas jet under it like a candle and I suspect it probably hasn't boiled yet. The MPs found Terry and Jock and brought them back. I won't say they were drunk as skunks, but they'd had a good drink. They'd booked us into a pensione in Fontainebleau so after meeting up, we slept the night and decided we'd travel so far, each day, stop and stay, taking two or three days to get to Cannes.

I did most of the driving and wore white cotton gloves because it was so hot and sticky. We stopped in Reims on the second day and, when we got back into the car, I couldn't find my gloves, so I said I'd have to go and buy some. My mother reminded me it was leap year – 1956. Astonished, I asked what that had to do with anything. She explained the Victorian custom when, if a woman asked a man to marry her, he'd say yes if he wanted to but, if not and to save embarrassment he'd buy her a pair of gloves. I turned round and said to Jock in the back seat, will you marry me? And he said yes! And we did. That was Sam. That was how I met my husband. He always said it was the dearest pair of gloves he'd never bought.

From then on, that was it. When we got to Cannes, walking along the front, he held my hand and when I hesitated, he said: 'Well, we are going to get married,' and we were married for almost sixty years before he died in April 2020.

We went abroad the next year too as Terry and Jock were still doing their National Service based at NATO. He'd always been known as Jock and until we put the banns up, I didn't know he was really called Samuel. His mother and father had a corner shop in Rutherglen, near Glasgow, Scotland. Sam's dad worked in a carpet factory from seven until 3pm and mum opened the shop then dad worked at nights until 9.00 pm. I don't think his mother ever forgave him for marrying a sassenach.

My sister did some research and traced Sam's family back to Dumfries where they were comb makers using shell and bone, which makes sense in the days before metal. or plastic combs. His grandfather's birth certificate spells his name as Raffle but on his death certificate it was Raphael. I guess they just couldn't spell.

We had got engaged with no proper plans. Sam came out of the Army with about eighteen months left of his five-year apprenticeship as a turner in Scotland. I was working at Evesham telephone exchange at the time, so asked if I could transfer to Glasgow and was warned it might take some time. There were advantages to being on the telephone exchange while we were living so far apart – I never minded getting up early so I was almost permanently on 7.00 am to 3.00 pm and quite often I'd do weekends too so, when it wasn't busy, I could phone and speak to Sam. We got engaged on 18 July 1960, and on 14 August I got my transfer. He met me off the night train and asked should we set a date for the wedding, so I said, in about six months. When we checked, it would be a

Tuesday and Valentine's Day. When I went back home, we put up the banns and I found out what his full name was. Our wedding was at the Methodist Church in Evesham. We were glad it was a Tuesday because Sam's parents were very busy at weekends and so were my parents.

My wedding day was ridiculously busy. Sam and his best man were staying with Daphne and David, who had married the previous Christmas Eve, so, at 7.00 am, I drove to pick up his mum, dad, Mr and Mrs Reston and Elizabeth who was a bridesmaid, from New Street station in Birmingham and came back to cook breakfast for us all.

Then Dad came in and asked if I could put on my wedding dress. I pointed out it was only 10.30 am and we were not getting married until 3.00 pm but he said Midlands Today were arriving at 11am to do wedding photos and wanted to film me coming across on the ferry as a bride. We phoned Sam, the best man, and the bridesmaids and page boy, then we all got dressed for our wedding photos, most were taken before the wedding. Photo shoot finished I went back upstairs and changed to serve the dinner for seven of us because my mum and Daphne were busy getting the reception ready at the Methodist church hall.

Finally dressed again, we set off for the church. Going down Bridge Street, as we were parked at traffic lights by the Town Hall, Dad said: 'I'm supposed to give you some pearls of wisdom at this time – father to daughter, but I really can't think of what to say.' 'The best advice I can give you is trust in the Lord and keep your bowels open!' I was still giggling when I got out of the car at the church. And we got married.

In those days you didn't have a big party at night. We'd booked

The wedding party crossing by Ferry for TV

And our official photograph later that day

the church hall but only until 6.00 pm so Mum was anxious in case people hadn't gone in time, but she needn't have worried. They had all rushed home to see the wedding on TV on *Midlands Today*.

A while before the wedding, my Aunt Edith said she knew we were going to London for our honeymoon but, as it was a long way to go after the wedding, she'd booked us a night at the Queen's Hotel, Cheltenham, as part of a wedding present. Dirk Bogarde was my favourite star at the time and his film *The Singer Not the Song* was due to open in London, so I'd booked tickets for the première on the Friday after the wedding.

Our wedding day turned out to be the hottest February ever recorded – my mother-in-law had bought a fur coat, but it was too hot to wear it. The bridesmaids had capes and muffs, which they couldn't wear either. So, on the Wednesday morning, Sam said even though we'd booked to go to London, he fancied going to the seaside from Cheltenham. And we went to Weston-Super-Mare, which was bright and breezy, and we loved it.

On the Friday we set off to London and saw the film. We had a bag of chips when we came out and then Sam apologised for asking, 'But have you got any money?' I thought I only had a couple of quid. He said the hotel was proving dearer than he'd thought and he didn't think we could afford both to stay and do anything else in London. So I said: 'OK – we'll go home tomorrow!' I'd had a week off work before the wedding and I had another week off too. Another plus to going home early was that it would give us time to see my family before we went back to Scotland to live.

We arrived home about 10.30 to 10.45 on the Saturday morning to find Dad doing the Ferry. He looked like death warmed up. I asked what was wrong and he said: 'The kids haven't turned up so I'm on the Ferry and I feel awful.' The café was closed too, because mum was poorly as well, so I went and opened the café and Sam took over the Ferry to the surprise of anyone who came in and thinking we were on our honeymoon.

The next Tuesday, we drove up to Scotland with Mum and Dad and Mr and Mrs Reston. On entering the house, I was surprised to see the table laid with a big cake on it, then realised that it was my twenty-second birthday, we had all forgotten, including me, my parents and my husband but my new mother-in-law had remembered... Then on the Friday, we had a reception for the Scottish side of the family of whom there were hundreds. Sam was an only child and so was his dad, but his mum was one of eleven. I couldn't keep up with all the cousins. She was a Russell with her own tartan and very proud of it. We had a wonderful party and we all enjoyed it very much

## Chapter Fourteen

# The 1960s – Life in Scotland and Back Home

I did enjoy living in Scotland and I was there for about twenty months in all – six months before we married and then for another year and a bit. I stayed with Mr and Mrs Morrison, Sam's best friend, Ian Livingstone was engaged to Betty Morrison and it was arranged that I would stay with her family until we got married.

Mr Morrison was an electrician working in the shipyard and he also played the bagpipes, being in great demand for weddings and funerals. They lived in high-rise flats, in Castlemilk and were on the on the second floor. Mrs Morrison, in her working life, had been in service, and she showed me round the flat: three bedrooms, large lounge, bathroom and a galley kitchen. She said I could go wherever I liked but not into her kitchen. If I wanted a drink, she would make it for me. I was still doing 7.00 am to 3.00 pm shifts and so I had breakfast in bed at 6.00 am, Mr M would go to work at 8.00 am and would get his breakfast in bed while Betty, who started work at 9.00 am, had the same service.

Mr Morrison said he'd been talking to someone in the pub who said Renfrew Borough Brass were looking for players, so we made an appointment to visit them, Sam took me in his dad's car. We walked in and the man started talking to Sam as if I wasn't there. Sam had to explain he didn't play but I did. His face was a picture – a lassie playing in the band! But he agreed to give me a trial and the upshot was I played with them for near enough eight months, and they were brilliant. Only one man made it obvious I wasn't welcome but only the one. They gave me an instrument, but I said to Sam I couldn't practice in the flat. I needn't have worried because Mr Morrison took me up on to the roof where he played his bagpipes, and I practised there too. There were four or five of these big buildings so no-one would have known where the sound came from.

I was enjoying working in the telephone exchange too, which I was told was the largest in the world. It was true when it was foggy you couldn't see from one end to the other of the switch room. It was on top of the shops in the complete block of Sauchiehall Street and Hope Street. There were ten operators on a team and if anyone was off sick or on holiday, I'd fill in. With about 110 girls, there were always collections for someone leaving or getting married. Everyone would put in a copper or two even if you didn't know them. I got to know so many that, when we got married six or so months after I'd started the supervisor said she couldn't believe the response – they all knew me!

This was long before subscriber dialling when you had to go through the operator. I'd spent weeks learning the Scottish codes and trying to understand the accents.

I remember taking a call from someone in a phone box, their number answered, and I told the caller to press button A, as he was through, but nothing happened. I repeated he should Press button A – nothing. I could not hear him but he could hear me so I asked him to Press Button B and then I would be able to hear him. He pressed button B and assured me he did not have a button A. I said of course he had, it was round the side of the coin box: 'Oh sorry, lassie', came his answer: 'my bonnet's hanging on it!'

I loved the accents and sometimes I didn't understand them at all. When we went back south, people were always asking Sam to say something because they loved his accent. I always said that's how we got married because I didn't understand what he was saying.

We left Scotland in the April of 1962 when our son John was a few months old and moved into the bungalow next door to Hampton Ferry. This had belonged to Frank Watkins and been converted into a café for the campers. Since the new cafe had been built, it was used to store things but when my parents knew we were coming back they made it into a home for us and we lived there with John.

The first Christmas, we went back to Scotland for New Year to see his family and friends and Sam said he'd really like to go back there to live, so we agreed to have a look round and see if there was anything we fancied. And we did look about. By this time, his mum and dad had sold their shop and, although his dad was still working in the factory, they both loved dancing and had joined a modern sequence formation team. We thought we'd be able to go out and they'd baby-sit but they were never in. They were in in the daytime to play with John but, four nights a week at least, they were out dancing.

Sam's friends came to visit us, but that New Year put paid to any idea of going back, mostly because here, when we wanted to go out, my Mum and Dad were around to baby-sit and Dad, especially, loved to come to our house to watch what he wanted on the telly. So that put paid to that. Our home and future was to be at Hampton Ferry.

Sam had loved his job but never went back to it. He worked

## Chapter Fourteen

at the Ferry and, in 1964, we became partners in the business. At first, he found it strange to work weekends, which had always been for football, which he loved. He played and was very good, so he made a bargain to do whatever was needed every other day, but Saturday was football.

First, he played for a team in Hampton. They did very well and were in the final of a couple of cups. They went to a cup final and, when he went to play, found they'd signed on two or three very good players who they were paying. Sam was very clear about what was right and what was wrong so when he saw money in their boots, he asked what it was for, and they replied they'd come to win the cup. As they'd come that far without help, he said he wouldn't play if they did. He packed his bag and that was that.

Through friends, he found Bretforton Old Boys and stayed with them the rest of his life. I sometimes wondered which was most important – me or Bretforton Old Boys. When he joined and played for them, they all had their own strip but wanted someone to wash them all. Sam collected about 6d a week from each player to pay for the washing and then, if they needed something like new footballs or a net, they'd put on an event and Sam would collect the money – in fact, becoming the treasurer.

They used to change in a garage but started talking about building something for the away team to use, so they built another garage next door. This not being big enough they eventually built Bretforton Club House, which they always called the Bug Hut, as the changing rooms had always been known. Now it's got a bar and all mod cons.

When I was mayor Sam asked if I'd go to one of their presentation nights, impressing the guys by getting the Mayor of Evesham to present the prizes. I was sitting nearby the bar and heard them talking and say: 'Well, we'll have to ask God.' I asked who's God? And was told it was 'your ruddy husband!' They wanted some new nets and would only get them if he said yes – so he had to be God. If it hadn't been for Sam, there wouldn't be the Bug Hut now. He'd tell them that, if they wanted something, they had to do something for it – hold an event, a special day or something. The cricket club was a separate club and so was the ladies' hockey club and held their own fund-raisers. He said this was silly. Why didn't they join to become Bretforton Sports Club. This was agreed if he would become treasurer, which he did, and this developed into a proper club house and all it entailed: wages, vat, insurance, lots of forms to fill in and he even started a Christmas club which was very successful. He loved doing it, and admitted he wished he had been an accountant.

## Chapter Fifteen
# A growing family then tragedy

After the war, Thomas Ellin, (Uncle Gus) from the BBC continued coming for his holidays every year and, when he retired, which was about the time we moved back to Evesham, he told Mum and Dad he'd like to stay while he was looking for somewhere to live nearby. He'd had a golden handshake of £20,000 as their chief cashier and, with a house then costing about £2,000 or so he would have plenty of choice.

Instead, he just stayed here and, I think, forgot to look... he died here seventeen years later.

He became part and parcel of the place and was a lovely man who'd do anything for you from washing, chopping wood, cleaning, if it didn't involve money. He was so incredibly tight, my dad said he'd skin a fart for a farthing. But he was always there to help. The milkman used to come to the town side and leave the milk in a box. Uncle Gus always put the empty bottles in it and brought the fresh milk in. He'd put the washing out and bring it in. He felt we were his family and I think, on the quiet, he really loved my mum.

And he was great with the kids. He'd ask if he could take the baby out and off they'd go in their pushchairs or whatever while he'd talk to them about anything and everything, the birds and the bees and the dandelions. They learned a lot from him.

We were living in the bungalow next door, which had previously

Sam and our three boys: John, Jamie and Scott.

converted into a café for the campers and then into a home for us. They put in a bathroom, and it had two bedrooms, a sitting room, kitchen and bathroom. We were very happy there. John liked it, then we had Jamie and Scott, our third son who was to die tragically in an event that re-shaped all our lives.

John and Jamie could swim but not Scott because in the winter it meant going to pools in Tewkesbury, Cheltenham or Worcester – an outing and a big effort but which we did at least once a week.

On 13 December 1968, the river was in flood. There was no fishing. Dad had gout and Sam was in bed with flu. My mum was up and pottering about. The older boys – John was seven and Jamie was five – went out to play football and, of course, Scott – who would have been three on 12 January – wanted to go with them. They were at the back of the house, but he got his bike out and we assume that, when he went round to the front of the house, with the river much nearer than usual, he must have tipped his bike over and fallen in. By the time we found him it was too late.

Up until then I'd never thought of anything but me, mine, and the Ferry but when we lost Scott, I thought this was something no-one else should have to go through. It was devastating. I said then it wouldn't have happened had I been able to take him swimming two or three times a week instead of just once a week he would have been able to swim. But, although he couldn't swim, he wasn't afraid of water.

So, as I will detail later, I joined the campaign that had started to get a pool in Evesham through Vespa – the Vale of Evesham Swimming Pool Association – and that was the start of my public life.

At the time, Dr Cox was very good to me and visited me most days for almost two weeks until he thought I could cope. He then advised us to have another child as soon as we could, he felt sure it would help. At first, we were doubtful, but decided that we would perhaps be better if we did have another baby. We had to wait until spring 1970 when I realised I was pregnant but when we told Mum and Dad in Scotland their reaction surprised us both. They had been devastated by the loss but next day, Mum phoned and asked us to look for a home for them. They said they were moving down to England to be near us and make sure that nothing like Scott's death happened again. They were putting their house up for sale and would move as soon as possible.

I told my parents and, when we went to Mum's and Dad's for lunch, Dad casually mentioned he had got us a house, with an appointment to view it at 4.00 pm that day. Sam and I were flabbergasted. Dad never left the place so how did he do it? He explained he had been talking to Mr Wilson who lived at 19 Boat Lane with his wife and small child, and was a market gardener with the ground from their house down to our meadow by the Ferry. His wife did not like living there as it was too quiet and she was lonely with no neighbours. So that day Sam and I went to visit them, looked at their house, liked it and made up our minds straight away we would have it. Agnes and Jack could live there and hopefully, when the time came, we could retire to there.

Sam phoned his parents and told them that we had found a house, and it was close enough to be very convenient, and if his dad wanted, E. W. Huxley & Son would employ him. Everyone was delighted and around August, they had sold their house and were moving to Evesham. A big step for them but they were both pleased and liked the house. Jack was delighted to work outside and loved the Ferry, quickly making friends with several of the caravaners. They also found several places where they could go dancing and saw the grandchildren every day, so everyone was pleased.

Our fourth son, Robert Wellesley Raphael was born at Evesham Maternity Unit on 8 November 1970.

## Chapter Sixteen
## Caravans, Fishing and a New Cafe

Soon, there were more caravans, and fishing was at its height. We couldn't take enough bookings; we hadn't got enough pegs. A club would book thirty pegs – we had 120 – so Mum would note them down like theatre seats. There were matches all the time. And then another ten would be booked for a day, which is when the camping really started – they'd come on Saturday and ask to stay over to Sunday.

Camping turning into caravans brought the problem of how to get them on site. We applied for a static caravan licence so you could only bring them on once. We had a licence for thirty caravans, and you had to go to the railway and tell them, then a man and a flag would come, and we'd bring one caravan on to the site, meaning it took two or three years to fill the site. We had prepared a back row and a front row and assumed the front would go first but it was the back row that went first. Now, everybody wants the front.

Back in the '60s, when Mum and Dad were doing well, they wanted to build a toilet block to replace the disgusting 'country closets' down the meadow. They got planning permission, but everything had to be delivered to the bungalow on the hill. Sam would go with the tractor and bring whatever it was down. We had the two children by this time, and they usually went everywhere with Sam on the tractor, if they could.

My dad, Ernest Huxley, in typical pose

One Sunday he went to get a load of breeze blocks into the trailer, which nearly creased him. As he came down the hill towards the level crossing and turned, the trailer tipped over and all the breeze blocks fell out. He felt the tractor going, so he just jumped off and the tractor went down the hill, up onto the Severn Trent Road where it teetered and went down the other side. He couldn't see it anywhere. All there was, was a caravan. The tractor had gone down the road and into the caravan, breaking the window and was then hidden behind the curtain. He had to ring the owner and tell him. But, as he always said, thank God I didn't have the kids with me.

So, we built the toilet block and had to install electricity and water. Wilmott & Fletcher in the Market Square were going to do it, so trenches were dug, plans made and the electric cable was delivered on a huge reel. The driver came down via the Severn Trent Road and stopped saying he would unload there so he could get the van out. Sam said he should go a bit further but he wouldn't listen. He got the huge reel off the trailer, pushed it onto the ground where it dropped with a thud, unhitched the van, and drove off.

It had been raining and was wet. And this huge reel started rolling. It rolled right through the gate down to where a man had been fishing before going for his lunch. It went over his creel and splashed into the river, just as the *Gaiety* came by full of people.

This was hundreds of pounds worth of cable. My brother was alive then and said he'd get it out. He got his tractor, a crowbar, and some chains, stripped off and went in with the crowbar. He pulled it through, chained it up and got it out. It hadn't been in the water for more than half an hour but couldn't be used. There was quite a song and dance over who should pay.

## Chapter Sixteen

The next time, the electrician was waiting and made sure it was put where it was wanted, by the toilet block. A great improvement. When Mum asked what we needed to do to increase our numbers, we were granted the new licence for seventy static caravans. So we went into the 1970s with fishing increasing and the caravan site doing well.

Meanwhile, our family was growing too. John, born in 1961, went to Prince Henry's Grammar School from Hampton School. He always loved acting and was involved in lots of things locally as well as working in the business from the age of eighteen to twenty-four, and circumstances changed. He decided he wanted to go to drama school and was accepted into Cardiff University as a mature student.

Jamie, born two years later, was always a practical lad and begged to go to Evesham High School but went to Prince Henry's with his brother. On reflection this was a mistake on our part, as John was academic and did well but Jamie was more practical, but Prince Henry's had only just become a comprehensive and he was always compared with John, which was not good. He left at sixteen and got a job as a trainee cook, which caused problems as it meant he couldn't play football as he had to work weekends. Then he became an apprentice bricklayer, which he enjoyed and which has stood him in good stead. Robbie, our youngest son, was born just as the fishing and caravanning were increasing. He went to St Egwin's and then Prince Henry's, following his brothers. He worked in the cafe at weekends and when needed but became a trainee accountant with Emsley & Co. Which he enjoyed and did very well. He left there when it was obvious we needed him in the business, for which we were both very grateful and he has been involved ever since.

Once again, we realised the cafe was too small. One of Sam's footballers was an architect so did the plans for a new cafe. The Interval had served its purpose and the Bright Interval was too small so it was time to build the Brightest Interval. We had hoped we would be allowed a two-storey building so Sam and I and our family could live in a flat above the café but planning was refused and it was back to the drawing board for a single storey building. On paper it looked good and we were pleased to get

The new cafe with three generations: Eileen Huxley, me and John Raphael, in 1978

them passed. The job was put out to tender and Chris Holmes from Broadway was selected as builder, doing a great job. On 18 October 1978, the Brightest Interval was opened coinciding with a fishing contest. Everyone was very impressed and particularly with the toilets, which were now indoors, clean and proper. When one of the anglers emerged he exclaimed very loudly that it is all wonderful and 'They have even got Welly Warmers.' Not quite understanding what he meant, Sam inquired and was told the warm air hand dryers were fantastic. Ever since, they have been known as Welly Warmers.

Our first effort catering for large numbers came quickly when we invited all the builders, plumbers, electricians involved to come for an evening with their husbands, wives and partners. We provided food, and tea and coffee but, with no licence yet for a bar, they brought their own alcohol. We all had a wonderful evening although we were shaken by the amount of washing up. I was also surprised and pleased when they presented me with a beautiful made trolley to help clear the tables – a unique gift.

We took down the old café and it was moved across behind Ferry House where we put in a pool table, table tennis, dart board, TV and an old three-piece suite for the boys. It became Hampton's unofficial youth club.

## Chapter Seventeen
## Into Public Life

As I mentioned earlier, my first involvement in public life was helping VESPA (Vale of Evesham Swimming Pool Association), as I was determined no-one should go through what we had. There had been a pool on the banks of the river Avon but that was only in the summer, and it was a bit grotty and hard to teach a load of kids. The town needed a proper pool. I'd been invited to join the town chamber of commerce a few months earlier, by Bob Turner from the NatWest bank.

Even though I'd only been to a few meetings, everyone was very sympathetic after Scott died and helped considerably in the campaign for a pool, offering to have an event or something to raise funds for Vespa.

The first time I went to a town council meeting I wasn't on the VESPA committee, but the swimming pool was coming up and we'd all been asked to lobby our councillors. I went to see mine and he agreed with me all the way.

We went into the council chamber where they started discussing whether a pool was necessary and if the money could be better spent elsewhere. There was a legal adviser who spoke for quite a long time and, to be quite honest, I couldn't understand what he was saying. Mrs Pitcher, the mayor, finally banged the table with her gavel and said: 'You've been speaking for five minutes, and I haven't understood a word you are saying.' We all clapped and cheered. In the vote, the only councillor against was the one I'd been to see. When I tackled him, he said he'd listened to everything but thought it was too much money. Can you put a price on a child's life?

I was involved with VESPA as well as the chamber of commerce, where tourism was a constant topic, although not properly appreciated by others in the late '60s. Two men from a fish and chip shop had been very keen to start a tourism association but only about four people came to their first meeting. But when it came up again in the 1970s, Bob Turner asked me if I would have a meeting in our café and thirty to forty came, including the most important man, Colin Garrett, Wychavon tourism officer. The owner of Leadon's caravan park in Broadway also came. They were 100 per cent behind it all.

By this time the chamber of commerce had become the Vale of Evesham Chamber of Commerce and Tourism Association although people still took some convincing. We'd just personally spent more than £11,000 to put electricity on our caravan park with a local firm but, when I asked them to join, they said tourism had nothing to do with them. I pointed out what we'd just had done and said, if that wasn't tourism, I don't know what was. The problem was, and still is, that some people just see tourists as a nuisance, taking their parking spaces, and ignoring the tremendous amount of money they bring to the town. But we were on our way, with Colin Garrett the first chairman and Leadon's' owner the first president.

My involvement with the council happened through George Emms, the *Journal* reporter, who used to come over the Ferry every day to go to work frequently asking if there was anything newsworthy going on at Hampton Ferry. If there was, we would tell him. One day he told me there was a bye-election due. Three people had been elected to represent Hampton in May but come October, as one had done nothing, not been to any council meetings, there was to be a bye-election in November 1984.

George asked if I'd thought about standing but I said I knew nothing about the council – I'd only even been in the office about once – so wouldn't know where to start. He said he'd take care of everything. And he did. He got the forms, the people to nominate me and assured me no-one else was standing. But, in the end, there were three of us including Pat Wilde, already a Wychavon District councillor who knew her way around, as well as being popular and pleasant.

I wanted to withdraw and said: 'That's it, Pat will get in.' But George persisted: 'If you work at it, you'll do it. You've got to go knocking on doors and I'll come with you.' He knocked on doors and introduced me. People said they knew me as I was 'Ernie's daughter', or because I was 'John's mum', even 'Deirdre's sister' . . . I went home hopping mad because no-one knew me and I thought I wanted them to know me, not someone's wife, sister, daughter but me. Sam was usually very quiet and rarely said much but when he did it was worth listening to. He'd said if standing for council was what I wanted to do that was fine and he would support me all the way.

I've always stood as an independent, not for a political party but, after the election nominations were announced the first people to come and see me were Martin Davey and John Smith, who asked if I'd stand as a Conservative. I said no because I didn't know enough about politics. All I cared about was Evesham.

## Chapter Seventeen

At the count, Pat Wilde's husband said to Sam: 'Your wife is rather splendid. I hope she doesn't get to upset by not winning.' That was like a red rag to a bull to Sam but he replied: 'Of course she'll win – she's been around and knows what she's doing.'

John and Martin had given me a lot of help and were at the count too, watching what was going on. Martin said that whatever I was told, I should ask for a recount, even if I won. When it was announced I'd won by three votes, he said ask for a recount, but I didn't need to because Pat did, and the outcome was that I'd got in by twenty votes. I'd won by a bundle – the number comes from a bundle of asparagus. Six bundles bound together is a round of gras. There should be twenty buds in a bundle and that's what I won by and so I became an Evesham Town Councillor.

They were very good to me and very patient. I had a call from the town clerk, asking me to go in to swear in. The briefing took a good two hours. I was told what was expected of me and what wasn't. I'd gone quite smartly dressed in a trouser suit, but he said: 'Just for the record, at Evesham Town Council the men wear the trousers.' I also learned there was a hierarchy of where to sit, with the last elected the furthest away. I would get the meeting's minutes and other papers to read through in advance and should phone the clerk if I didn't understand anything.

If I wanted to speak, I had to put my hand up for the mayor to acknowledge and would have to wait if more than one person wanted to speak. When called, I had to stand behind the chair and speak for no more than two minutes, I couldn't come back into the conversation unless someone asked a question only I could answer. Now, I'm glad to say, that's all gone out – no two-minute rule and it's not just men who wear the trousers.

I was also told that, if I had to go out on council business before 5pm, I was to wear a hat and carry gloves. After 5pm if it would be suitable, I could wear a tiara. I came home and told Sam I had to buy a tiara. He was not impressed.

The town clerk then, Mr Caldicot was wonderful – he'd been on the borough council before it became Town Council in 1974 and what he didn't know about Evesham wasn't worth knowing.

I don't think I spoke at council for a good three or four meetings but after the first I attended I was invited to join everyone at the Royal Oak. I went, even though I had to tell them I didn't drink, everyone was very friendly and came up and spoke to me.

The swimming pool was still an issue when I joined the council – it was going to happen, but we didn't believe it really. Then, another issue I was concerned with, was to do with a man who had a garage along Waterside and who kept a little cabin cruiser boat. One night he came up the river at an alarming pace, at about 11–12.00 at night and tried to go straight through the Ferry rope, which pushed him back. He called my dad all the names under the sun and said there should be a light on it. Dad said, as he understood the local bylaws, you shouldn't move a boat after dusk – and this wasn't dusk, it was dark! Within a short time, they were replacing old gas street lighting with electric, I was quite pleased to have street lighting in Boat Lane.

## Chapter Eighteen
# Promoting Evesham

I was still involved with VECTA, and we advertised in the *Birmingham Post* and *Evening Mail* that we'd provide free coach travel for two people from any club organising outings, to come to Evesham for the day. We asked the mayor to give them coffee in the town hall and we gave them £2 vouchers each to spend in town on food or drink. They could also go round the museum for free. We met up at 2pm in the park and took a boat trip down to Chadbury and back in time for afternoon tea at Raphael's.

The coach took them to Twyford where they were all given a small basket of plums and sent them on their way. It was a huge success, and trips were organised for many years afterwards, and brought many people to Evesham to spend a pleasant day,

I had become a tour guide in 1979. There was a course at Evesham College and cocky me thought I'd just roll up and get my badge, as I knew such a lot – the arrogance of youth! It was brilliant. There were ten on the course, which involved going a day a week for ten weeks and we learned all sorts of things. At the end, the lecturer asked if we had thought about becoming a tour guide and the group agreed to set up Evesham Tour Guides – the first in the town. We would take it in turns on Tuesday afternoons to take people on a walking tour round town.

From there it just grew and got bigger with coach tours. Dudley Coaches would advertise them, doing four tours. It started when the blossom was out and, a year or two later the Asparagus Tours were added and then, several years later, plum tours were organised.

Dudley's Coaches picked up from, several places including Gloucester, Worcester and Birmingham and then picking up the tour guides from the Valley. My personal favourite was the Asparagus Tour we would step on the bus at The Valley then we'd go to the Fleece for coffee, drive round to look at people cutting asparagus, go to Evesham museum and see some of the history and sometimes I did a tying demonstration there, then we stopped for lunch in town. We did an asparagus lunch at Raphael's, from soup to asparagus hot or cold in a salad and we even had asparagus ice cream. Many of them would join us for lunch.

Then, leaving from Hampton Ferry we went to Revill's farm, which is now the largest grower in Britain which does white, green, and purple asparagus. They didn't have a restaurant when we started only a small tearoom. Arrangements were made for Eckington Manor's chef to give a talk and demonstration on how to serve asparagus: grilled for ten seconds with butter and garlic, fresh in salad or boiled, as most of us do. Yes, it was possible to have a taste which was always great. Then we'd take them back to Twyford (now known as the Valley) where they could go round and do some shopping if they wanted before they left for their return journey home.

People came from all over the country – it was very popular. We would start at approx 10.30 am and finish at 4.30 pm. A lovely day out. The asparagus season runs from 23 April, St George's Day, until midsummer day on 21 June. And, in that time, if we spot anyone selling imported asparagus and not local, we shout at them and jump up and down. Angela Tidmarsh, Wychavon's tourism officer, would go round asking shops to buy from Mexico or Peru in the winter but not in season. Now asparagus has been registered for Evesham. And Billy Bird from Bretforton had to be the best man to tie a round of gras which he did all his working life, sadly he died in 2023. He was old school, and much appreciated for his skill. Now, at Revill's, in Defford, it grows flat not up and over the mound. How times change.

When I was four or five, we had asparagus growing at the Ferry and we would get up at 4.00 or 5.00 am to cut it. My father and brother went up the rows and they could get two pieces of asparagus in between their fingers and make a fan, so they could hold quite a lot of asparagus in their hands. When they got to the top of the row, they'd put it down and my sister would pick it up and put it in her doll's pram and take it back to my mother, who was running the Ferry and tying the asparagus. And I'd pick it up from the other end of the row and take it to Mum too. If we weren't on the Ferry with the asparagus tied on a trolley, for the 8.20 am train to go to Smithfield Market, we were late for school.

Mum very rarely made a round of gras because it had to be woven with willow. She'd sometimes be asked to, but dad had to buy the willow, and he didn't like that. He planted six willow trees on the opposite bank of the river but by the time the willows grew, the asparagus beds had gone to make way for the caravans, but the willow trees are still there. The asparagus beds used to go all the way up to the white bungalow.

But the first guided tour we did for visitors was to see the blossom and we still do those, then the asparagus as well as the plum tours and we are trying to do more. Wychavon's tourism officer, Angela, does it all as well as setting up tours from Twyford with step-on tour guides. Our driver was often asked by other coach drivers where the tour guides came from so this started a new venture where we get on a coach and take them on a tour.

There's also have someone who does a mediaeval tour, about once a year, with a mediaeval breakfast, which takes people to the site of the battle of Evesham and another popular one is the Archers, for people who listen to the radio programme – there are about four of these a year, but it varies.

## Chapter Nineteen
# Twinning with USA

We started our twinning links with New Jersey in the United States of America in the late 1970s, when Evesham, New Jersey had an income tax bill meant for Evesham, England. The bill was sent back by their town clerk who commented she hadn't realised there was an Evesham in England. So, our town clerk, Peter Gordon sent back leaflets, with thanks for the bill and that was that.

Roll forward to 1988/89 and Evesham, New Jersey was celebrating being three hundred years old. That's considered old in America, with Chicago only celebrating being a hundred years old that year. Evesham Township decided to mark their anniversary with an event every month, starting in the January with a special ball, inviting all the local businesses to have a table and to sponsor an event during the coming year: one a month sponsored by a different company each sponsor usually with an interest in the event like sport, art, photography, music.

It was suggested Evesham in England should be invited, not expecting anyone to go but hoping for a card or something. The invitation was for the ball and eight of us on Evesham Town Council accepted, which put them in a frenzy. However, they asked through the churches for hosts and were inundated. It was suggested we went two days before the ball and stayed on afterwards, so we were hosted for two weeks. I stayed with Tom and Kitty Rovito, and during this time together, we talked about twinning, which they didn't know as it was a European idea that had grown out of the friendship between a French soldier and a German prisoner-of-war during WW1. They set out to encourage the idea after the war, reasoning it would be very difficult to go to war again and fight your friends.

The American hosts took us everywhere, even the State capital, where they arranged for us to sit in a session. In a big park we found a plaque on a tree about Quakers who had meant to dock in New York but, because of bad weather, sailed on up the Delaware River, stopping in what is now Evesham, New Jersey. The party of Quakers had met in Evesham, UK staying in the jail, not in a hostelry because they didn't imbibe of the grape. And when they went to America, they took local names with them: Bretforton, Camden and many more so we felt quite at home.

There is no town of Evesham, but there are Evesham schools, Evesham police and Evesham Town Council, and hospitals. It is an Area called Evesham Township and the main town is Marlton, if you want to find it on the map.

Evesham, England was already twinned with towns Dreux in France, Melsungen in Germany, and as a town were being encouraged to twin with Todi in Italy. We talked about twinning with Evesham USA, and they were all for it so wheels were set in motion during this trip.

The ball itself was incredible and was very special. We had evening dress and went in a stretch limo to a huge office block of many storeys. On the ground floor, there was a four-or five-piece orchestra playing, while canapés and drink were served in the huge foyer. There were lifts all the way down on both sides and soon it was announced we should go up in the lifts to the next floor.

## Chapter Nineteen

Here, the tables were laid for dinner with perfect silver service. A delicious three-course meal was served. Then coffee was served upstairs, and we found sofas and coffee tables for two hundred or so people, as there were speeches and thank you.

If you wanted to dance the night away, it was upstairs again, and this was marvellous. We watched and chatted and even talked to William Penn, and Benjamin Franklin, two of our hosts in perfect period dress and totally in character, a fascinating encounter.

Then, when it was time to go home, we took the lift or walked down again to find that everything had been cleared away and you'd never have known anything had been there. A fantastic evening, which I will always remember.

Thanks to our twinning friendships I've been able to link travel with my other passion for music.

I was asked to be President of Avonbank Brass Band several years ago and, although not playing any more, I have enjoyed many concerts and have helped when and where I could. I was honoured to be made the Mayor of Evesham in 1990 and the mayor usually has named charities, raising funds for them during their year. I made Avonbank Training Band one of my charities. Years later when Avonbank Band was celebrating its sixtieth anniversary, I arranged for the band to visit our twin town in the USA. It was eventful and wonderful and memorable.

One event that will remain with me for the rest of my life was when we played in the shopping mall one afternoon. It's a huge place and the band were to play in the entrance foyer. Now, the evening, before several of the players had been to a match final, where the 'Phillies' had won the cup for first time in twenty-seven years, and you can imagine just how exciting that was.

So our band are playing in the mall where there are lots of people listening and others just walking by when the conductor announces they are going to play *The Post Horn Gallop*.

He raises his baton to start, looks to the soloist – and sees an empty chair. Someone points up stairs. To the left, there is an escalator going up and to the right of the balcony there is an escalator coming down. There's Steve Lane, the soloist, on the balcony and ready to play. The band starts and the crowd parts to let Steve walk along the edge of the balcony to reach the down escalator. He steps on and goes down, playing the *Post Horn Gallop* all the time. He reaches the bottom and steps towards his seat, where he plays the last note. He could not have timed it any better if he had practised for months.

Instructed to take a bow by the conductor he bends down and puts on a 'Phillies' Cap, bowing to the people who have now gone quite wild. I suspect the screaming was not only because of his brilliant playing but also because he wore the cap. It was marvellous. Twinning was a great experience and one I have been very grateful for.

## Chapter Twenty
## Mayor-Making, Wellies and Blooms

Every February the town council has a meeting with no minutes or notes to decide who's going to be the next mayor and the deputy mayor. It was always done on seniority and they never went back down the list. One year, we were on holiday when they had the meeting. Roger Spragg was next in line and agreed to be mayor, but at the next meeting, he said he couldn't do it after all, so it was my turn. This hadn't crossed my mind and there were some who thought I wasn't capable but Peter Gordon, the then Town Clerk, said I was next in line. I went home and told Sam they'd asked me to be mayor, but I would need a consort. He said if it was what I wanted he'd do it, but only for one year. Now, as a child, I remember if anybody fell in the river they were pulled out and addressed as 'Your Worship, the Mayor'. This tradition came from the early 1800s when, in the pub now called Ruby Jack's, they complained the mayor never came from down Bewdley Street, so in a drunken stupor, they held their own election. They would put someone in a wheelbarrow and push him down the street. If he managed to stay in the wheelbarrow they'd tip him in the river, pull him out and call him 'Your Worship, the Mayor.' I said at mayor-making I was glad this method of election was no longer used.

Quite often we had remarks from people about how lucky we were to live in such a lovely place, which of course was true, but on one occasion Sam and I were crossing the river in five foot flood, going to a posh dinner in full evening dress covered in raincoats and wearing wellingtons and as he rowed the boat he remarked: 'We are so lucky to live in a lovely place like this.' I could not help but smile.

We couldn't have vehicles on site as I've said because of the access but after this I wrote to Severn Trent and said there would

Mayor of Evesham

be times I couldn't get out to engagements if the river was in flood, so they said I could have access to use as I saw fit. So this saved me having to cross the river again in a rowing boat on my way out in evening dress to a Mayor's Ball or charity dinner when the river was in flood. I had an amazing time as mayor, going to so many wonderful places and meeting wonderful people but this was an unexpected benefit.

We went to lots of things as mayor and Sam was my consort. Two or three years after my year we went to a funeral and Sam wore his suit again, which he didn't like doing if he didn't have to, but I saw his shoulders shaking with laughter. He pulled out of his pockets a mountain of raffle tickets that we'd bought at the events we'd been to!

As mayor from 1990 to 1991, I wanted to do something to beautify Evesham so I asked Peter Gordon, the town clerk, if we could enter Britain in Bloom. He said all you had to do was enter, which he did for several years, it was when Frank Green became town clerk and he was given a criteria that we found out how much was involved. I wanted to start with hanging baskets round the town hall and market square, but we had to apply for planning permission for each lamppost and that cost most of our £500 budget.

We had the sensory garden and the Almonry Gardens looked good too but until now, we did not know there was a criteria. The judges had just come and gone. Now we found they wanted young people involved, they wanted to see new buildings and restored buildings and so on. They wanted everybody to be involved. With VECTA, Clive Allen and I had organised our own Evesham in Bloom for two or three years with all sorts of categories. We'd

Meeting Princess Anne, now the Princess Royal, when she visited Evesham. Reproduced courtesy of the *Evesham Journal*, Newsquest.

Also meeting Princess Margaret. Reproduced courtesy of the *Evesham Journal*, Newsquest.

never seen the judges but when we got the new criteria it changed everything.

We'd also been to the awards for a few years and knew we'd never get far because in our category of medium town were also Stratford-on-Avon, Droitwich, Leamington Spa, and Warwick. We always came last, with Droitwich next to last but we were determined to pull out all the stops and, at least, beat Droitwich. When we got there, Frank said we couldn't have won because we were on a table right at the back of the hall with the Alcester team and he felt sure that the winners would have been seated nearer to the presentation area.

We should have known better as Alcester won their category almost every year. We'd all sent in photographs with our entry and were just sitting there, hoping to beat Droitwich, when this woman said: 'Look it's your picture of the Almonry Gardens' and we were gob-smacked to be third! Stratford always came first. They'd been left some money to enhance Stratford – rumoured to be thousands of pounds, so they always won. One of the judges of Britain in Bloom lived in Evesham and, the year 2000, we went to the presentation and thought Stratford had won again but they didn't, it was Evesham I asked this judge, whether we had really won or was it that Stratford lost? He told me we had won because we had stuck to the criteria like glue and covered everything that we were asked.

Evesham has great natural advantages with the river and so much land. Most of the area belonged to the Rudge Estate: Crown Meadow, Corporation Meadow and our family land is all Rudge. They were an important family. John Rudge was born the same day as my dad and, because his dad was squire, the bells rang so my dad always said the bells rang for his birth. John Rudge married and had four girls. When his wife died, he later married again and had four boys. When he died, his estate was shared between his wife and his eight children

This was almost the first time anything had been sold. They lived at the top of Greenhill in the Abbey Manor, a big house, which was sold for housing. The Rudge Estate includes the park and all the land by the Almonry Museum. There's quite a story behind the Abbey gardens. Three men were discussing putting two gardens at the top of Abbey Park to commemorate the wars, using the Sebastopol cannon from the museum. They asked permission from the town council, were told it came under Wychavon, but: 'You'd have to ask the Rudge Estate.'

One of the men had been at university with Edward Rudge, so he arranged to have lunch with him and his wife, to explain the idea, which Edward said sounded good. However, his wife intervened and asked why they were only asking for two small bits of a garden when you could have a lovely park up there. This was not what they'd been expecting but that's where the wonderful Abbey Gardens have come from. It's now being restored to help bring it to life for visitors to imagine how it would have been when the monks lived there. The Rudge Estate has said they would transfer the land to the Abbey Trust, which has wonderful plans, and it's been agreed that Wychavon District Council will maintain it when all the legalities have been sorted and when it is satisfactorily finished.

## Chapter Twenty-One

## Times of Change

On 1 December 1978, we held my parents' golden wedding celebration for family and friends with an open invitation for any of the ferry boys that would like to come and see Mum and Dad again. One of the ferry boys was Stan Raye who was now a jet-setting chief executive for Tannoy. He'd been evacuated to Evesham during the war and had been a part-time Ferryboy, meeting my parents during his two-year stay in Evesham.

My brother said a few words and proposed a toast to Mum and Dad, Stan then asked if he could say a few words. He said how much he had enjoyed his time in Evesham and that they had influenced him so very much, that, when he was faced with a difficult decision, he would say to himself: 'Now, what would Mr and Mrs Huxley do.' He said it helped him considerably, and he was grateful that he knew Mum and Dad, who had always had time to answer the questions of an inquisitive boy.

What surprised Deirdre and me even more was that he and his wife had found the time to come as they lived in London and travelled a lot. They had expected to be in the old, cold café, so had put on long johns and woolly jumpers. A truly memorable evening was had by all.

Dad had Parkinson's disease, but he wasn't particularly unfit and still managed to do a lot of things. When they bought the railway and built the Severn Trent Road, Dad asked if we could

My parents' golden wedding with their Ferryboys

Sam and me with our three boys: John, Jamie and Robert

contribute to it to give us access to the caravan park, as before we had to notify the railway. But they sent him away with a flea in his ear and said he would never go on that road.

On 21 January Dad died in his sleep, aged seventy-five. Mum discovered him that Sunday morning and said we must send for an ambulance or a doctor. The doctor pronounced him dead and sent for the undertaker. And which way did the undertaker come? The irony of it was, down the Severn Trent Road. And even my mum laughed at that. She said Dad would have loved that – they told him he'd never use the road, but he did.

Sam's parents were still in Boat Lane and, by the time Dad died, we had swapped house, moving from the bungalow into the Ferry House. Mum still knitted and sewed even with terrible arthritis in her hands, all lumps, and bumps everywhere. She'd say: 'It's not going to beat me.'

But, a year after Dad died, Uncle Gus died, and that meant Mum was living on her own. We thought she was probably not eating well so she moved in with us and we made her room in the Lounge. That was the first we knew of the story of how they'd lived when they moved there, and she said she'd come full circle.

Mum played bridge and Sam loved cards too, so she taught him to play and he became the only man I know who took his mother-in-law out three nights a week to play contract bridge, at the Chateau Impney, Droitwich or in Worcester or in Broadway. Mum would come home and say I'm not very popular tonight. I asked how she knew, and she said, if I do something wrong, he calls me Mrs Huxley. And if I do something right it's well-done short arse!

She played right up to the end. She lived with us for a good six months but died nine days after her eightieth birthday. A lot of people wanted to see her for her birthday, but she got so tired that my sister arranged for them to come one at a time, have a cup of tea in the café, then over on the Ferry and spend time with her. We had quite a party in the café with so many people there and it was a lovely day. Mum appreciated she had visitors, almost a family at a time, but did not know that Deirdre had arranged it all.

Then a few days later she had a stroke and was taken to Evesham Hospital in Briar Close where she died on 6 June 1984.

In 1986 Sam and I celebrated our silver wedding with a seven-week journey of a lifetime. We did not think that we would be able to afford it but all the family chipped in for our travel costs to Australia where our best man and his wife were working in Melbourne. They got married three weeks after us so we went to visit them for their silver wedding.

When trying to book our flight most of the airlines allowed only one stop each way and we could not decide where we would like to stop. I had been given a card when visiting the World Travel Market in London and told to contact him when we knew when we where we were going, and he would get us the best price possible. So I did and he said we could stop as often as we wished as long as were going in the same direction. We went from London to Washington, then to Los Angeles, on to Hawaii and then Melbourne where we stayed with Betty and Ian for three weeks, from there we went to Sydney to visit my cousin, had three days in Fiji, then turned round and made our way home via Hawaii, San Francisco, New York and then back to England. The total air fare for the two of us and Robbie was £2,028. A truly fantastic, once in a lifetime holiday.

## Chapter Twenty-One

Jamie had been an apprentice bricklayer and this had finished just as we got back off our holidays, so he decided to take time out and visit Australia for six months – and loved it. When he came back, he got a job at Cox & Co as a bricklayer and bought a house in Hampton that needed doing up and then married Joanne. Barry, his best man had gone with his job and moved to Australia, asking them over for his fortieth birthday on Bondi Beach. Their daughter Lauren was born in 1990 and, when she was thirteen, after visiting there they decided to move to Australia. Lauren is now married to Simon and has two children, beautiful daughters Remi and Ottilie

From drama school, John had had a long-time girlfriend who went on to become a well-known actress Raki Ayola, that did not work out and he met Rachel back in Evesham, with whom he had a son. He worked for CBG in Blackminster and astonished everyone by being able to talk to some of the European drivers in their own languages.

Sam was taken ill and diagnosed with angina, which meant he had to slow down and take things easier We decided it would be best to sublet the café which took up most of our time. We made sure it was all done legally and got a tenant for the café while we managed the caravan site, fishing and the Ferry – so no more late nights and early mornings for us. It all went well for two years and then, unexpectedly, they left at the end of September, just before the huge Fort Dunlop fishing contest which brought down more than two hundred people – one of our busiest Saturdays – and we got the keys to the café back the Sunday before.

Jamie was in Germany, working as a bricklayer with three others and John was in London, managing a pool hall during his university holiday. Jamie's wife Joanne rang them and said: 'Come home. Your parents need you.' Robbie got time off from his accountancy training and even his boss Joan Emsley came to join the work force.

The place was stripped out, cleaned, decorated. The loos were disgusting, and the plumber poured cola syrup down them and by next morning they were they were pristine. It was all done by the Friday for the competition on Saturday.

And so we stayed on in the café, with help for the heavy lifting. Robbie came to manage the café in 2003–4, which made life much easier. One of our Ferry boys Bryn had been at catering college and came to work for us before heading for London. He soon came back and has been with us ever since. He married his partner David who also is a chef, but trained as a horticulturist first and still loves plants and flowers, with Braves Plants now becoming established at Hampton Ferry. Dad would have been pleased as this is how he started.

Sam and I had a happy marriage and we never fell out or argued. We agreed to differ but Sam would never argue with me. If he thought we were going to argue he would just agree with me, which was most annoying but there was nothing I could do about it. On one occasion I gave Sam the silent treatment at breakfast and asked one of the children to pass the marmalade, the response was, why not ask Dad he is closer than me. I said I was not speaking to his Dad. Sam replied: 'Thank God for that. I thought I had gone deaf.' We all laughed and that was the end of that.

Sam did not enjoy good health during the last three years of his life and finally spent time in hospital. He was transferred from Redditch to Evesham Austen Care Home in March 2020 as Covid

## Chapter Twenty-One

A new boat in 1984 and the old ferry was filled with flowers

hit the country so my biggest regret was that I could not visit him for the last three weeks of his life. I do hope he did not think I had abandoned him. He died on 1 April 2020.

On our fiftieth birthdays twenty years earlier we had purchased a plot in Hampton Cemetery where we wanted to be buried when the time came, thinking it was easier to discuss then rather than leave it until later. I asked him what he wanted in the way of hymns, or perhaps a piper and in which church would he like the service. His response was typical Sam: 'Oh don't bother with that – just dig a hole and throw me in.' Which because of COVID is almost what we did. I think he would have liked it.

## Chapter Twenty-Two

# Reflections

I served thirty-five years on Evesham Town Council and enjoyed it all very much, I did not stand for election when Sam was ill, but of course remain very interested in the town of Evesham. Our youngest son Robert is still on the Town Council and is also on Wychavon District Council, becoming chairman in 2020. COVID meant he could do very little so he was offered the chairmanship in 2021–22 which was still a bit slow because the country was still recovering from COVID. And in May 2023 he was asked if he would like to do chairman again, which he agreed asking me, as he needed a consort. What a year it proved. Wychavon DC celebrated being fifty in May 2024 and, between May 2023 and 2024 the chairman was asked to visit all the parish councils in the district – all seventy-seven of them. I have been his consort some of the time and Cllr Marion Griffiths has helped when it involved too much walking or standing, so I went where it was sitting and eating – it worked out well.

It has been an exciting year. I had no idea Wychavon was so full of interesting, wonderful people. I have enjoyed it very much but not as much as Robert, who has done everything asked of him. I am very proud of him and I am sure his father would have been too.

In May 2024 he was made mayor of Evesham with Cllr Marion Griffiths is his mayoress. He knows the family are proud of him and will help him all they can.

We've been here ninety-five years this year and I think we must be one of the oldest small family-owned businesses left in Evesham. They say mum and dad start it, son or daughter increase it and the grandchildren sell it. So far things have worked out well. When Sam died in 2020 my youngest son Robert was already working with us and had been made a partner. He is unmarried, so who takes over in the family next? I do have two grandchildren. Lauren, Jamie's daughter and Alexander, John's son, so I have high hopes of it continuing.

The years since 1929 have seen many changes but we are still here at Hampton Ferry and have grown and expanded, hopefully, given our customers what they want. Menus change, as do expectations. We are fortunate in having a wonderful staff, who I feel love Hampton Ferry as much as I do and I trust we will be here as a business for a few more years yet. In 2029, God willing, we will be celebrating one hundred years in business in the beautiful town of Evesham.

It has been a privilege to have lived at Hampton Ferry and have loved living next door to Paradise. Looking back over the years I think of the warmth and friendship, the sense of family that we've known and that gives me enormous confidence for the future of Hampton Ferry. We've had tragedy in our lives and so much happiness too. Dad was right . . . we really do live next to Paradise.

*Next to Paradise*, photograph by Daniel Davies, November 2021